KEY MATHS

Foundation

GCSE

▶ **Chris Humble**
▶ **Fiona McGill**

First published in 2001 by
Nelson Thornes Limited
Delta Place
27 Bath Road
Cheltenham GL53 7TH

01 02 03 04 05 / 10 9 8 7 6 5 4 3 2 1

A catalogue record for this book is available from the British Library.

ISBN 0-7487-3394-9

The authors are grateful to the following examinations boards for permission to reproduce questions from their past examination papers. (Answers included have not been provided by the examining boards, they are the sole responsibility of the authors and may not necessarily constitute the only possible solutions.)

London Examinations, a division of Edexcel Foundation (UCLEAC/Edexcel)
Northern Examinations and Assessment Board (NEAB)
Associated Examining Board (SEG)
Welsh Joint Education Committee (WJEC)

The publishers have made every effort to contact copyright holders but apologise if any have been overlooked.

Artwork by Oxford Designers and Illustrators
Cartoons by Clinton Banbury
Typeset by Wyvern 21 Ltd, Bristol, UK
Printed and Bound in Spain by Graficas Estella S.A.

Contents

Introducton

Key Maths GCSE Foundation Revision Book has been developed as an invaluable revision resource for thorough preparation for Foundation GCSE. Written by experienced authors with years of classroom experience, this book supports and enhances work done with the **Key Maths Foundation GCSE Pupil Book**.

A number of features are included to help you with your foundation revision and preparation.

- Each separate section covers the four core areas of the National Curriculum for Number, Algebra, Shape, space and measures and Handling data.

- Each section has an opening page identifying the key areas to be covered for ease of use.

- Every page comprehensively covers the key areas you need to study and revise. A notes section provides additional support and reminders where appropriate.

- **Unit 13** pages 301–305 These are provided to indicate where a particular topic is covered in the main pupil book. You can use this to refer back to the particular unit and page number in the pupil book.

- See also These show you where related or additional material is available within this book for extra practice.

- Test Yourself questions are provided after coverage of each core topic. These allow you to practice and gain confidence as you work through the book.

- At the end of each main section there are a range of actual examination questions for you to try. These allow you to test your understanding for each of the four core areas.

  Revision books for Intermediate (ISBN: 0 7487 3395 7) and Higher (ISBN: 0 7487 3396 5) are also available.

Visit our extensive website at **www.nelsonthornes.com** for additional mathematics resources and materials to support your work.

1 Number

- [ ] **Place value**
- [ ] **4 rules of number**
- [ ] **Types of number**
- [ ] **Negative numbers**
- [ ] **Fractions**
- [ ] **Percentages**
- [ ] **Linking fractions, decimals and percentages**
- [ ] **Ratio**
- [ ] **Rounding**
- [ ] **Changing currencies**
- [ ] **BODMAS**
- [ ] **Standard form**

Practice questions

To change a decimal to a percentage you just multiply by 100!

Place value

☐ Whole numbers

You write numbers in columns.

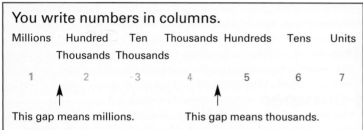

Millions	Hundred Thousands	Ten Thousands	Thousands	Hundreds	Tens	Units
1	2	3	4	5	6	7

This gap means millions.   This gap means thousands.

You group the digits in 3s from the right with gaps between.

The number is one million, two hundred and thirty four thousand, five hundred and sixty seven.

Example

Write this number in figures.
Two million seven hundred and nine thousand and four.

Leave a gap after you write the figure for millions.
Leave a gap after you write the figures for thousands.
Two million, seven hundred and nine thousand and four.

The number is 2 709 004

☐ Decimals

Units	Tenths	Hundredths	Thousandths
7 .	6	5	4

The values get bigger as you go to the left.

☐ Putting numbers in order of size

To put numbers in order of size, look at one place at a time.

Look at the numbers before the decimal point first.

27.352   24.398 is smaller than 27.352
24.398   because 24 is smaller than 27

If the numbers before the decimal point are the same keep looking right until the numbers are different.

6.976   6.976 is smaller than 6.985
6.985   because 7 is smaller than 8

Example

Put these numbers in order of size. Start with the smallest.
2.392, 2.329, 2.356

In order the numbers are 2.329, 2.356, 2.392

2

☐ Multiplying by 10, 100 or 1000

> To × by 10, move all the digits one column to the left.
> To × by 100, move all the digits two columns to the left.
> To × by 1000, move all the digits three columns to the left.

Examples

Work out 42×10

Th	H	T	U		42
	←	4	2		× 10
	4	2	0		= 420

Notice how the 4 and 2 both move one place to the left.
Fill in any spaces before the decimal point with 0s.

Work out 62.37×1000

TTh	Th	H	T	U	t	h		62.37
←	←	←	6	2 .	3	7		× 1000
6	2	3	7	0				= 62 370

Notice how the 6, 2, 3 and 7 **all** move three places to the left.
You need to fill in the units column with a zero.

☐ Dividing by 10, 100 or 1000

> To ÷ by 10, move all the digits one column to the right.
> To ÷ by 100, move all the digits two columns to the right.
> To ÷ by 1000, move all the digits three columns to the right.

Examples

Work out $14.5 \div 100$

T	U	t	h	th		
1	4 .	5				$14.5 \div 100$
→	→	. 1	4	5		= 0.145

Notice how the 1, 4 and 5 **all** move two places to the right.

Work out $249 \div 1000$

H	T	U	t	h	th	
2	4	9 .				$249 \div 1000$
→	→	→	. 2	4	9	= 0.249

TEST YOURSELF

1 Write these numbers in words.
   a 8945   **c** 204 097
   b 40501   **d** 7 400 076

2 Write these numbers in figures.
   a Two hundred and fifty four thousand seven hundred and twenty nine.
   b Three million two thousand and four.

3 Put these numbers in order of size. Start with the smallest.
   a 492, 37, 4091, 347, 429
   b 29.457, 29.375, 29.357

4 Multiply these numbers by 10.
   a 27   **b** 7.61   **c** 423.56

5 Multiply these numbers by 100.
   a 32   **b** 2.509   **c** 24.82

6 Multiply these numbers by 1000.
   a 68   **b** 8.073   **c** 36.8

7 Divide these numbers by 100.
   a 79 000   **b** 42 900   **c** 6007

8 Divide these numbers by 1000.
   a 43 000   **b** 24 700   **c** 6091

☐ Multiplying by multiples of 10, 100 or 1000

> Multiply the non-zero digits at the beginning of each number.
> Count all the zeros. Put these on the end.

Notes

Digits are the figures in a number.

Example

Work out: **a** 52×30 **b** 400×6000

a Do $\begin{array}{r} 52 \\ \times 3 \\ \hline = 156 \end{array}$ Count the zeros.

There is one $= 52 \times 30$

So $52 \times 30 = 1560$

b Do $4 \times 6 = 24$

Count the zeros. There are five. 400×6000

so $400 \times 6000 = 2\,400\,000$

The digits at the beginning of the numbers in example **a** are 5 and 3.

The digits at the beginning of the numbers in example **b** are 4 and 6.

Unit 7 page 169

☐ Dividing by multiples of 10, 100 or 1000

> To work out $800 \div 40$
>
> Cross **one** zero out on the 40
>   this divides the 40 by 10.
> Cross **one** zero out on the 800
>   this divides the 800 by 10.
>
> Then you have $8\,0\,\cancel{0} \div 4\,\cancel{0}$
>
> Then do $80 \div 4 = 20$
>
> ($8 \div 4 = 2$ and put the 0 on the end).

You look at the number after the divide sign to see how many zeros you can cross off.

Unit 7 pages 168, 170

Example

Work out $50\,000 \div 2000$

You can cross out three zeros on each number.

So $50\,\cancel{000} \div 2\,\cancel{000} = 50 \div 2 = 25$

Always cross out the same number of zeros on each number.

TEST YOURSELF

1 Multiply these numbers by: (1) 50 (2) 70.

a 20	**b** 30	**c** 50
d 15	**e** 42	**f** 67

2 Multiply these numbers by: (1) 300 (2) 6000.

a 20	**b** 400	**c** 670

3 Divide these numbers by 30.

a 150	**b** 600	**c** 930
d 1500	**e** 4500	**f** 6600

4 Divide these numbers by 400.

a 1600	**b** 6000	**c** 92 000

4 rules of number

☐ The 2, 5 and 10 times tables

The numbers in the 2 times table are all the even numbers.	$1 \times 2 = 2$ $2 \times 2 = 4$ $3 \times 2 = 6$ $4 \times 2 = 8$ $5 \times 2 = 10$	$6 \times 2 = 12$ $7 \times 2 = 14$ $8 \times 2 = 16$ $9 \times 2 = 18$ $10 \times 2 = 20$
In the 5 times table the numbers all end in 5 or 0.	$1 \times 5 = 5$ $2 \times 5 = 10$ $3 \times 5 = 15$ $4 \times 5 = 20$ $5 \times 5 = 25$	$6 \times 5 = 30$ $7 \times 5 = 35$ $8 \times 5 = 40$ $9 \times 5 = 45$ $10 \times 5 = 50$
The 10 times table is easy. Just put a zero on what you multiply by 10.	$2 \times 10 = 20$	$7 \times 10 = 70$

☐ Other times tables

The 9 times table can be done by using your fingers.

You can get the 4 times table by doubling the 2 times table. So you can do 6×4 like this; $6 \times 2 = 12$ then $12 \times 2 = 24$.

You can get the 8 times table by doubling the 2 times table twice. So 7×8 can be done like this: $7 \times 2 = 14$ then $14 \times 2 = 28$ then $28 \times 2 = 56$.

You need to know the 3 times table:	$1 \times 3 = 3$ $2 \times 3 = 6$ $3 \times 3 = 9$ $4 \times 3 = 12$ $5 \times 3 = 15$	$6 \times 3 = 18$ $7 \times 3 = 21$ $8 \times 3 = 24$ $9 \times 3 = 27$ $10 \times 3 = 30$

You can get the 6 times table by doubling the 3 times table.

This only leaves the 7 times table – you'll have to learn that!

You only need to know half your tables.
You only need to remember the ones with the smaller number first.
This is because 7×3 is the same as 3×7.

Notes

The 2, 5 and 10 times tables are really important. You can get other tables from these.

For example, the 4 times table is just the 5 times table take away the 1 times table.

You can do $4 \times 7 = 5 \times 7 - 1 \times 7$
$= 35 - 7$
$= 28$

Also the 9 times table is just the 10 times table take away the 1 times table.

You can do $9 \times 8 = 10 \times 8 - 10 \times 1$
$= 80 - 8$
$= 72$

Unit 4 page 85

You can do the 3 times table by doing your 2 times table and adding the 1 times table on top.

So $5 \times 3 = 5 \times 2 + 5 \times 1$
$= 10 + 5$
$= 15$

It is   7, 14, 21, 28, 35, 42, 49, 56, 63, 70

Unit 4 page 87

TEST YOURSELF

1 Write out these tables up to × 10.
Use any method.
a 6   **b** 7   **c** 8   **d** 9

2 Draw out a 10 × 10 tables square.
Remember you only need to work out half of it to fill it all in!

☐ Adding whole numbers

> To add numbers together put the digits in columns. Keep the numbers in the columns underneath each other.

Example

Work out 478 + 65.

H	T	U
4	7	8
	6	5
5	4	3
1	1	

8 + 5 = 13 so put the 3 in the units column and carry the 1
7 + 6 + 1 = 14 so put the 4 in the tens column and carry the 1

☐ Subtracting whole numbers

> When you subtract numbers put the digits in columns.
> Again, keep your columns straight.

To work out 673 – 469 set the sum out like this.

H	T	U
6	⁶7	¹3
4	6	9
2	0	4

You can't take 9 from 3.
So you take a ten from the column on the left.
Now subtract in each column.

☐ Multiplying whole numbers

> To long multiply you need to do it in 3 stages.
> To work out 263 × 74 first you work out 263 × 4

```
  2 6 3
×     4
─────────
1 0 5 2
  2 1
```

Do 3 × 4 = 12 and carry the 1.
Do 6 × 4 = 24 add the 1 to make 25 and carry the 2.
Do 2 × 4 = 8 and add the 2 to get 10.

Then you work out 263 × 70 on the next line.

```
    2 6 3
×    7 4
─────────
  1 0 5 2
1 8 4 1 0
1 9 4 6 2
```

This is 263 × 4.
Do 263 × 70 on this line.
Do the total on this line.

Lastly, add 1052 to 18410 to get the answer 19462.

Add each column to get the answer.
Don't forget the 'carries'!
Check each sum as you do it.
You should always check you wrote the question down correctly.

Leave a little space between each column to fit any little figures in.

The 7 becomes 6 and the 3 becomes 13

A 1 taken from the tens column becomes an extra 10 units in the units column.

A 1 taken from the hundreds column becomes an extra 10 tens in the tens column.

There are some other ways of doing long multiplication.

Box method
Here you do it like a times table square

X	200	60	3
70	14 000	4200	210
4	800	240	12

Then you add everything up:
14 000 + 4200 + 210 + 800 + 240 + 12
= 19 462

or there is this method:

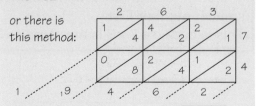

Do as a times table. So 2 × 7 =
Put a zero in any empty sections. Add the diagonals.
Carry into the next diagonal when needed.

☐ Dividing whole numbers

To work out 582 ÷ 3	
1	First do 5 ÷ 3. This is 1 with 2 left over.
3)5 ²8 2	Put the 1 above the 5 and carry the 2.
1 9	Now do 28 ÷ 3. This is 9 with 1 left over.
3)5 ²8 ¹2	Put the 9 above the ²8 and carry the 1.
1 9 4	Now do 12 ÷ 3.
3)5 ²8 ¹2	This is 4. Put this above the ¹2.

☐ Long division

To do long division, you need to work out some times tables for the number you divide by.

Example

Find 840 ÷ 24

24)8 4 0   First do 84 ÷ 24.

To do this you need to work out the 24 times table

$1 \times 24 = 24$
$2 \times 24 = 48$
$3 \times 24 = 72$
$4 \times 24 = 96$ 96 is too many so stop.

$24 \times 3 = 72$ so 84 ÷ 24 = 3 with 12 left over.

       3
24)8 4 ¹²0   Put the 3 above the 4 and carry the 12.
       Now do 120 ÷ 24.

You need to carry on the 24 times table.

       3 5 $5 \times 24 = 120$ so 120 ÷ 24 = 5.
24)8 4 ¹²0   Put the 5 above the zero.

Notes

Divide each number in turn.
Always carry any remainders.

You can show all your working out under the division like this:

```
        3 5
24) 8 4 0
    7 2
    1 2 0
    1 2 0
    0 0 0
```

There is another method called repeated subtraction if you find this way difficult.

To do 840 ÷ 24 take away as many 24s as you know you can do. Do this in stages.

```
    840
  − 240    10 × 24 = 240
    600
  − 240    10 × 24 = 240
    360
  − 240    10 × 24 = 240
    120
  − 120     5 × 24 = 120 do as    24
    000  35                       × 5
                                 120
```

So 35 lots of 24 go into 840.

TEST YOURSELF

1 Work these out:

  a 245 + 325 + 402
  b 72 + 467 + 5021
  c 203 + 4916 + 7278
  d 8799 + 2069 + 28 + 672

2 Work these out:

  a 379 − 234
  b 452 − 73
  c 283 − 167
  d 4025 − 888

3 Work these out. Show all your working.

  a 432   **b** 629   **c** 2756   **d** 3789
      × 3   × 4   × 6   × 7

  e 205 × 52   **f** 764 × 83   **g** 4597 × 89

4 Work these out. Show all your working.

  a 2)234   **b** 6)378   **c** 7884 ÷ 9

  d 23)276   **e** 8190 ÷ 35   **f** 5963 ÷ 89

☐ Adding and subtracting decimals

> When you do this: (1) keep the decimal points in line
> (2) fill any gaps with zeros.

Notes

Examples

Work out: **a** 2.45 + 3.7 **b** 4.7 − 0.32

a
```
    2.45       5 + 0 = 5
  + 3.70       4 + 7 = 11, carry 1
    6.15       2 + 3 + 1 = 6
    1
```
Put a zero in these gaps.

b
```
    4.⁶7̶¹0      You cannot do 0 − 2, so take 1
  − 0.32       from the column on the left.
    4.38       Then 6 − 3 = 3 and 4 − 0 = 4
```

Follow the normal rules for addition and subtraction.

3.7 is the same as 3.70

☐ Multiplying decimals

> The number of decimal places in the question is the same as in the answer.

Otherwise follow the normal rules for multiplication.

Examples

Work out: **a** 3.24 × 4 **b** 0.8 × 2.73

a
```
    3.24       There are two decimal places
  ×    4       in the question so there are
   12.96       two in the answer.
       1
```

b
```
    2.73       There are three decimal places
  × 0.6        in the question so there are
   1.638       three in the answer.
```

Do not try to keep the decimal points in line in this type of question and answer. It isn't necessary.

▶ **Unit 6** page 129

☐ Dividing decimals

> To work out £73 ÷ 5 do this.
>
> ```
>   14.60
> 5)73.³00   put these zeros in to continue dividing.
> ```
>
> Answer £14.60

Do as for whole number division. You just put a decimal point on the end of the whole number part of the answer. Keep the decimal points in line. Remember that your answer is in pounds and pence so you put the zero on to show the 60 pence.

TEST YOURSELF

1 Work these out.

    a 3.27 + 6.21
    b 4.85 + 5.2 + 0.08
    c £5.22 + £44.50 + £0.92
    d 246.89 kg + 40.09 kg + 0.056 kg

2 Work these out.

    a £4.92 − £2.37 **b** 5.6 m − 2.96 m

3 Work these out. Show all your working.

    a 2.54   **b** 74.29   **c** 1.74   **d** 419.8
       × 3   × 6   × 0.8   × 0.09

    e 3.67 × 1.2 **f** 22.8 × 0.36 **g** 0.045 × 9.8

4 Work these out. Show all your working.

    a 2.86 ÷ 2 **b** 59.01 ÷ 7 **c** £516 ÷ 8

Types of number

☐ Even numbers and odd numbers

Some lists of numbers follow rules.

These are called sequences.

One of the simplest sequences is the even numbers.

| 2 | 4 | 6 | 8 | 10 … |

You can show these as a pattern of shapes.

●　　●●　　●●●　　●●●●　　●●●●●
●　　●●　　●●●　　●●●●　　●●●●●

Another simple sequence is the odd numbers.

| 1 | 3 | 5 | 7 | 9 |

You can also show these as a pattern of shapes.

●　　●●　　●●●　　●●●●　　●●●●●
　　　●　　　●　　　　●　　　　●

☐ Multiples

These are simply times tables.

The multiples
of 3 are 　　3　　6　　9　　12　　15 …

Which are the
3 times table 　1×3　2×3　3×3　4×3　5×3 …

 Algebra **patterns** 　 page 34

☐ Factors

You can divide these exactly into another number.

These are all the factors of 24. They can be written out like this so you don't miss any.

| 1 | 2 | 3 | 4 |
| 24 | 12 | 8 | 6 |

So the factors of 24 are 　1, 2, 3, 4, 6, 8, 12, 24.

☐ Prime numbers

These only divide by themselves and 1, so they have only 2 factors. 1 itself is **not** a prime number. It only has 1 factor.

The first eight prime numbers are
2, 3, 5, 7, 11, 13, 17, 19

2 is the *only* even prime number.

The rule for this sequence is add 2.
These are also the multiples of 2.
The dots … mean the sequence can go on forever…!

There are other patterns as well,
e.g. for even numbers you could use:

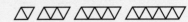

The rule for the odd numbers is also add 2 but these are not the multiples of two.

There are different patterns for the odd numbers as well.

The multiples of 3 are normally shown as

| 3 | 6 | 9 | 12 | 15 … |

You can draw patterns for these as well.

○　　○ ○ ○　　○ ○ ○ ○
○ ○　　○ ○ ○　　○ ○ ○ ○ ○

The multiples of 7 are 7, 14, 21, 28, 35 …

Factors are always whole numbers.
The smallest number that goes into 24 is 1.
The first pair you write down is 24 and 1.
The next smallest number that goes in is 2.
2 goes in 12 times so you write down 12 and 2.
You keep going like this until the factors 'cross over' 4 × 6 = 24 and 6 × 4 = 24 but you only need to write one 4 and one 6 down.

Prime numbers can only be shown by a rectangle with a width of 1, e.g. 7.

All other numbers can be shown as a rectangle where the width is more than 1, e.g. 15 is not a prime number because it can be shown like this

3 [grid 3 × 5] 5

☐ Triangle numbers

The triangle numbers are a triangular pattern of shapes.
You can make them by adding the whole numbers together.

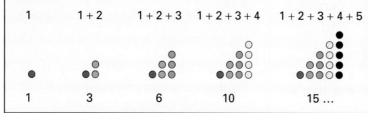

Each pair of triangle number neighbours make a square number.

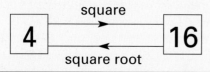

☐ Square numbers

You make these by multiplying numbers by themselves.

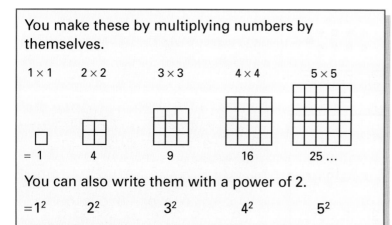

You can also write them with a power of 2.

$= 1^2$ 2^2 3^2 4^2 5^2

You should know your square numbers up to at least 10^2

You can use the $\boxed{x^2}$ key on your calculator to find a square.

☐ Square roots

To find a square root you have to undo a square.
So because $4 \times 4 = 16$ the square root of 16 is 4.
You can think of it like this

square
$\boxed{4}$ ⟶ $\boxed{16}$
square root

You do the opposite of squaring to find a square root.

You can use the $\boxed{\sqrt{}}$ key on your calculator to find a square root.

TEST YOURSELF

1 List the following sets of numbers:

   a the even numbers between 15 and 27
   b the odd numbers between 324 and 336
   c the multiples of 6 up to and including 36
   d the multiples of 9 between 32 and 64
   e the factors of 20
   f the factors of 36
   g the prime numbers between 30 and 40
   h the triangle numbers between 20 and 50
   i the square numbers between 40 and 130.

2 Look at these sets of numbers. Pick from this list the best words to describe them or to fill the spaces: **prime numbers, triangle numbers, multiples, factors, square numbers, square root, even numbers, odd numbers.**

   a 7, 11, 13, 17, 19   **b** 9, 12, 15, 18, 21
   c 6, 10, 15, 21, 28   **d** 49, 64, 81, 100
   e 1, 3, 6, 9, 18   **f** 8, 10, 12, 14, 16
   g the ___ of 144 is 12   **h** 51, 53, 55, 57, 59

Negative numbers

☐ Putting numbers in order

These are the bank balances of the Ardup family:

Carolyn –£40, Chris –£55, Stan £15, June –£25

Looking at a number line you can see who has most money.

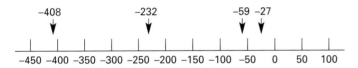

```
       Chris     Carolyn    June                          Stan
         ↓          ↓         ↓                             ↓
  ┼────┼────┼────┼────┼────┼────┼────┼────┼────┼────┼────┼────┼────┼────┼────┼
 −60 −55 −50 −45 −40 −35 −30 −25 −20 −15 −10  −5   0   5  10  15  20
```

OVERDRAWN ┆ cREDIT

The amounts in order of size are: –£55, –£40, –£25, £15.

Example

These are some depths below sea level: –232, –59, –408, –27.
Write them in order of size. Start with the lowest.
Think of where these would be on a number line.

```
        −408              −232              −59 −27
          ↓                 ↓                ↓   ↓
  ┼────┼────┼────┼────┼────┼────┼────┼────┼────┼────┼────┼
−450 −400 −350 −300 −250 −200 −150 −100  −50   0   50  100
```

The answer is –408, –232, –59, –27.

☐ Using a number line for calculations

Example

Doug works in tunnels. He starts from 75 m underground and goes up 45 m. Find his new position.

You can write the calculation like this –75 + 45.
You can then sketch a number line to show you what to do.

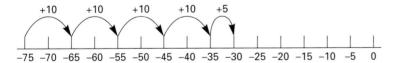

```
   +10    +10    +10    +10    +5
  ⌒      ⌒      ⌒      ⌒      ⌒
 ┼────┼────┼────┼────┼────┼────┼────┼────┼────┼────┼────┼────┼────┼────┼────┼
−75 −70 −65 −60 −55 −50 −45 −40 −35 −30 −25 −20 −15 −10  −5   0
```

He is now 30 m below ground. So –75 + 45 = –30

Doug then remembers he has left a spade 35 m below.
How far below ground is the spade?
You can write the calculation like this –30 –35.

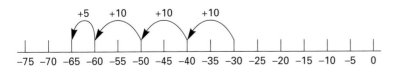

```
      +5    +10    +10    +10
     ⌒      ⌒      ⌒      ⌒
 ┼────┼────┼────┼────┼────┼────┼────┼────┼────┼────┼────┼────┼────┼────┼────┼
−75 −70 −65 −60 −55 −50 −45 −40 −35 −30 −25 −20 −15 −10  −5   0
```

Doug is now 65 m below ground. So –30 – 35 = –65.

The further you go to the left on a number line, the less the numbers are.

The further you go to the right on a number line, the greater the numbers are.

On this number line, Stan has the most money and Chris has the least.

The more negative a number is, the less it is. The closer to a positive number it is, the greater it is.

The number line in the example is horizontal, but you can use a vertical one.

You can think of –75 + 45 as down 75 from zero followed by up 45.

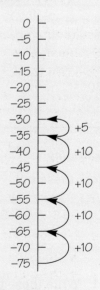

You can think of –30 – 35 as down 30 from zero followed by down 35.

☐ Adding with negative numbers

You can have two signs next to each other in calculations.

Andy has two store cards that he owes money on. He owes £30 on his Fred Bewis card and £25 on his Roofmart card.
He wants to know what his total overdraft is.

You can write this as a calculation −£30 + −£25

You can see there are two signs together.
Think of amounts he has to pay out in £10 and £5 notes.

−£10						−£10
−£10		−£10				−£10
−£10	+	−£5	=			−£10
						−£10
						−£10
						−£5

so   −£30   +   −£25   =   −£55

Adding a negative number is the same as taking away.

☐ Subtracting with negative numbers

Andy wants to pay off the money he owes. He can only afford to pay £40 back this month. You can think of this as taking money away from the amount he owes.

−£10						−£10
−£10		−£10				−£5
−£10	−	−£10	=			
−£10		−£10				
−£10		−£10				
−£5						

so   −£55   −   −£40   =   −£15

Subtracting a negative number is the same as adding.

Examples

Work these out: **a** 7 + −3   **b** 4 − −8   **c** −2 − +6

a 7 + −3 = 7 − 3 = 4   **b** 4 − −8 = 4 + 8 = 12
c −2 − +6 = −2 − 6 = −8

Notes

This shows + − together equal −

This shows − − together equal +

There are 4 possibilities with + and − together in 'double signs'. These are
++   +−   −+   −−

The rules for these can be shown like this.
++
──   } like signs together give +

+−
−+   } unlike signs together give −

TEST YOURSELF

1 Write these temperatures in order of size. Start with the lowest.

−11 °C,   −6 °C,   −53 °C,   −162 °C

2 Write these depths below ground in order. Start with the furthest below ground.

−409 m,   −2086 m,   −4099 m,   −206 m,   −208 m

3 Work these out. Show all your working.

a −5 + 3   **b** 4 − 6   **c** −3 − 7
d −16 − 7   **e** −1 + 3   **f** 34 − 49

4 Work these out. Show all your working.

a 7 + −4   **b** −12 − +4   **c** −14 − −9
d −22 − 16   **e** −19 + −28   **f** −198 + −467

12

Fractions

☐ Finding fractions of quantities

Look at this apple.
Taking a half of this is the same as dividing it by 2.

So if you want to find $\frac{1}{2}$ of a number you divide by 2.

To find $\frac{1}{3}$ of a number you divide by 3.

To find $\frac{1}{4}$ of a number you divide by 4.

Examples

Find: **a** $\frac{1}{3}$ of 18   **b** $\frac{1}{5}$ of 345

$$\qquad\qquad\qquad\qquad\qquad\qquad \overset{6\ \ 9}{}$$

a $\frac{1}{3}$ of 18 = 18 ÷ 3 = 6   **b** $\frac{1}{5}$ of 345 = 5$\overline{)3\ ^34\ ^45}$

In the fraction $\frac{3}{4}$ the top number is 3.
This means that there are 3 lots of $\frac{1}{4}$ in the number.
So to find $\frac{3}{4}$ of a number (1) divide it by 4
                                 (2) multiply by 3.

Examples

Find: **a** $\frac{3}{4}$ of 20   **b** $\frac{4}{5}$ of 235

                                           $\overset{4\ \ 7}{}$

a $\frac{1}{4}$ of 20 = 20 ÷ 4 = 5   **b** $\frac{1}{5}$ of 235 = 5$\overline{)2\ ^23\ ^35}$

     Then 5 × 3 = 15   Then 47 × 4 = 188

☐ Top heavy and mixed fractions

This is 1 whole pack 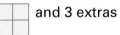 and 3 extras
of 4 yoghurts

Each individual yoghurt is $\frac{1}{4}$ of the pack.

So there are $\frac{7}{4}$ here altogether. This is a top heavy
fraction.

But you can also write this as $1\frac{3}{4}$. This is a mixed
fraction.

Examples

a Write $2\frac{3}{4}$ as a top heavy fraction.
b Write $\frac{9}{2}$ as a mixed fraction.

a $2\frac{3}{4}$ looks like this

There are 11 quarters here. So you write this as $\frac{11}{4}$.

b $\frac{9}{2}$ looks like this   So it is $4\frac{1}{2}$.

Notes

To find $\frac{1}{7}$ of a number you divide by 7 and
so on.

Unit 2 pages 33–34

The top of a fraction is called the
numerator.
The bottom of a fraction is called the
denominator.

You can also use a calculator to work
these out.
For $\frac{4}{5}$ of 235 key in

Answer: 47

Unit 2 page 37

Top heavy fractions are also called improper
fractions. You need to know this.

There is another way to do these.

With $2\frac{3}{4}$ there are 4 quarters in each of the
2 whole ones. Then add the 3 extras on.
So 2 × 4 + 3 gives 11 quarters = $\frac{11}{4}$.
There are 2 halves in each whole one. So
divide the 9 by 2 to find how many whole
ones there are. The one left over is the
extra $\frac{1}{2}$.

☐ Equivalent fractions

Look at this tray of raspberries.
There are 8 cartons in a tray.
So each carton is $\frac{1}{8}$ of the tray

 is the same number
of cartons as

so a quarter is the same as two eighths of a tray

You can write $\frac{1}{4} = \frac{2}{8}$

These are called **equivalent** fractions.
They are the **same** fraction shown in different ways.

You can make equivalent fractions by multiplying.

To change $\frac{3}{4}$ into eighths,

you need to make the bottom number 8

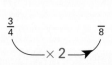

You multiply the
bottom by 2 to get 8.

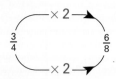

Then you multiply
the top by 2 to get 6.

You may find it helps to see the $\frac{1}{4}$ shown like this.

You can check these are the same on a calculator.

$\frac{1}{4}$ = [1] [÷] [4] [=] *0.25*

$\frac{2}{8}$ = [2] [÷] [8] [=] *0.25*

Equivalent fractions have the same value but are shown in different ways.

Unit 10 pages 232–4 ➤

What you do to the bottom of a fraction, you must do to the top.

Examples

a Change $\frac{1}{2}$ into sixteenths   **b** Change $\frac{4}{5}$ into hundredths

a

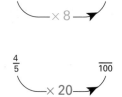

b

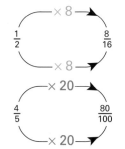

You always multiply the top and bottom by the same number.

T E S T   Y O U R S E L F

1 Work each of these out:

    a $\frac{1}{2}$ of 22   **b** $\frac{1}{3}$ of 21   **c** $\frac{1}{4}$ of 36

    d $\frac{1}{5}$ of 45   **e** $\frac{1}{6}$ of 48   **f** $\frac{1}{7}$ of 49

    g $\frac{1}{8}$ of 72   **h** $\frac{1}{25}$ of 200   **i** $\frac{1}{12}$ of 360

2 Work each of these out:

    a $\frac{2}{3}$ of 21   **b** $\frac{2}{3}$ of 36   **c** $\frac{3}{4}$ of 24

    d $\frac{2}{5}$ of 25   **e** $\frac{3}{5}$ of 50   **f** $\frac{4}{5}$ of 380

    g $\frac{5}{6}$ of 72   **h** $\frac{8}{9}$ of 756   **i** $\frac{4}{25}$ of 800

3 Write these as improper (top heavy) fractions:

    a $1\frac{1}{2}$ **b** $2\frac{2}{3}$ **c** $3\frac{3}{4}$

    d $3\frac{2}{5}$ **e** $4\frac{5}{6}$ **f** $4\frac{15}{16}$

4 Write these as mixed fractions:

    a $\frac{11}{2}$ **b** $\frac{14}{3}$ **c** $\frac{22}{7}$

5 Make these fractions equivalent:

    a $\frac{1}{2} = \frac{}{8}$ **b** $\frac{3}{8} = \frac{}{16}$ **c** $\frac{4}{5} = \frac{}{10}$

    d $\frac{3}{7} = \frac{}{14}$ **e** $\frac{14}{25} = \frac{}{100}$ **f** $\frac{8}{9} = \frac{}{360}$

☐ Cancelling fractions

You can cancel fractions by **dividing**.
Look at the top and bottom of the fraction.
If they are in the same times table you can divide both by the same number.

Notes

Here both 4 and 8 are in the 4 times table. So both 4 and 8 will divide by 4.

☐ Adding and subtracting fractions

To + or – fractions the bottom numbers must be the same.

So $\frac{1}{8} + \frac{5}{8} = \frac{6}{8}$ and cancelling down

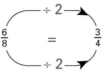

When the bottom numbers in fractions are different, you must make the bottom numbers the same.
You do this by using equivalent fractions.

What you do to the top of a fraction, you must do to the bottom.

$$\frac{1}{8} + \frac{5}{8} = \frac{6}{8} = \frac{3}{4}$$

Example

$\frac{15}{16} - \frac{3}{4}$

First change $\frac{3}{4}$ into sixteenths

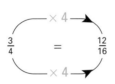

Then subtract as normal $\frac{15}{16} - \frac{12}{16} = \frac{3}{16}$

You add mixed fractions by adding the whole numbers first.
You subtract mixed fractions by making them improper.

You always multiply the top and bottom by the same number.

5	10	15	20	
4	8	12	16	20

Examples

a $1\frac{4}{5} + 5\frac{3}{4}$ **b** $2\frac{5}{6} - 1\frac{2}{3}$

a $1 + 5 = 6$ then $\frac{4}{5} + \frac{3}{4} = \frac{16}{20} + \frac{15}{20} = \frac{31}{20} = 1\frac{11}{20}$

    then add these two answers: $6 + 1\frac{11}{20} = 7\frac{11}{20}$

b $2\frac{5}{6} - 1\frac{2}{3} = \frac{17}{6} - \frac{5}{3}$

         $= \frac{17}{6} - \frac{10}{6} = \frac{7}{6} = 1\frac{1}{6}$

The lowest number that 5 and 4 both divide into is **20**. So you make both $\frac{4}{5}$ and $\frac{3}{4}$ into twentieths.

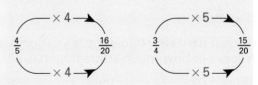

TEST YOURSELF

1 Cancel these fractions down:

   a $\frac{2}{4}$ **b** $\frac{6}{8}$ **c** $\frac{10}{16}$

   d $\frac{4}{16}$ **e** $\frac{3}{12}$ **f** $\frac{6}{9}$

   g $\frac{5}{20}$ **h** $\frac{10}{25}$ **i** $\frac{8}{24}$

2 Work these out:

   a $\frac{1}{4} + \frac{1}{4}$ **b** $\frac{3}{4} - \frac{1}{4}$ **c** $\frac{5}{8} + \frac{7}{8}$

   d $\frac{13}{16} - \frac{3}{16}$ **e** $\frac{5}{6} + \frac{5}{6}$ **f** $\frac{4}{5} - \frac{1}{5}$

   g $\frac{6}{7} - \frac{4}{7}$ **h** $\frac{5}{8} + \frac{1}{8}$ **i** $\frac{5}{12} - \frac{1}{12}$

3 Work these out:

   a $\frac{3}{4} + \frac{1}{2}$ **b** $\frac{3}{4} - \frac{5}{16}$ **c** $\frac{5}{8} + \frac{7}{16}$

   d $\frac{3}{5} - \frac{3}{10}$ **e** $\frac{5}{6} + \frac{2}{3}$ **f** $\frac{4}{5} - \frac{3}{20}$

   g $\frac{3}{4} - \frac{7}{12}$ **h** $\frac{2}{5} + \frac{5}{8}$ **i** $\frac{5}{7} - \frac{4}{9}$

4 Work these out:

   a $2\frac{1}{4} + 1\frac{1}{2}$ **b** $3\frac{1}{2} - 1\frac{5}{16}$

   c $5\frac{1}{3} + 3\frac{5}{6}$ **d** $4\frac{4}{5} - 1\frac{3}{10}$

   e $6\frac{3}{4} + 2\frac{4}{5}$ **f** $7\frac{1}{7} - 5\frac{2}{3}$

Percentages

☐ Writing percentages

> Percentages are just another way of writing hundredths.
>
> So you can write $\frac{7}{100}$ as 7% and $\frac{89}{100}$ as 89%
>
> Percentages add up to 100%.
>
> So if you spend 60% of your money there will be 40% left.

Example

June scores $\frac{68}{100}$ in an exam.

a Write her mark as a percentage.
b What percentage of the exam did she get wrong?

a She scored 68%

b 100% − 68% = 32%
  She got 32% wrong.

☐ Finding a percentage of an amount

> To work out 60% of £240:
> (1) Write the percentage as a decimal.
> (2) Multiply the quantity by the decimal.
>
> 60% = 0.6   then
> $$\begin{array}{r} 240 \\ \times\, 0.6 \\ \hline 144.0 \end{array} = £144$$
>
> or using a calculator
>
>   Answer £144
>
> **Fractions** page 13, **Linking fractions** page 20

Example

Stefan earns 8% interest per year on his savings of £585. Work out how much interest he has after 1 year.

8% = 0.08   then
$$\begin{array}{r} 585 \\ \times\, 0.08 \\ \hline 46.80 \end{array} = £46.80$$

or using a calculator

   Answer £46.80

See also ▷ **VAT** page 18

Notes

This is 1%. It is 1 square out of 100.

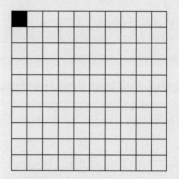

It is not very much!
That is because $1\% = \frac{1}{100} = 0.01$

In the square above 1% is shaded. This means that 99% isn't shaded.

With simple percentages you may find it easier to use fractions.
So to find 50% of £250 use $50\% = \frac{1}{2}$
then $\frac{1}{2}$ of £250 = £125
The percentages you should be able to use fractions with are:
50% (finding a half)
25%, 75% (finding quarters)
10%, 30%, 70%, 90% (finding tenths)
20%, 40%, 60%, 80% (finding fifths)
$33\frac{1}{3}\%$, $66\frac{2}{3}\%$ (finding thirds)

Your calculator will display *46.8*
Don't forget that it is money so you must write a zero on the end to give £46.80.

☐ Percentage increase and decrease

In the last example you saw how to find 8% of £585.
Suppose you then have to find what Stefan has altogether.
You have to add the £46.80 interest on top of the £585.
This gives a final total of £585 + £46.80 = £631.80.

You can use a percentage to find an increase in an amount.
There are two steps:
(1) Find the percentage of the quantity.
(2) Add it on to the amount you started with.

The amount at the start is £585.

The 8% increase is £46.80.

The final amount is £631.80.

Example

Ian pays £450 for a mower.
He sells it for 20% more than what he bought it for.
Work out how much he sells it for.

Step 1   20% = 0.2   then
$$\begin{array}{r} 450 \\ \times\,0.2 \\ \hline 90.0 \end{array} = £90$$

or key in ⬛ 0 ⬛ . ⬛ 2 ⬛ × ⬛ 4 ⬛ 5 ⬛ 0 ⬛ = ⬛   Answer £90

Step 2   Amount at start + increase = final amount
             £450   +   £90   =   £540

Ian has made a profit on this mower.

A 20% gain is a 20% profit.
You may be asked to find the profit in a question. This will be the increase.

You could do this by using fractions.

$20\% = \frac{1}{5}$ then $5\overline{)450}$ = 90

A quick method is to find 120% of £450.
100% is the £450 amount you start with.
The 20% is the increase
120% = 1.2 then £450 × 1.2 = 540

To find a percentage decrease:
(1) Find the percentage of the quantity.
(2) Take it away from the amount you started with.

A decrease is the same as a reduction.
A loss is also a decrease.

A quick method is to find 76% of £2680.
100% is the £2680 amount you start with.
24% is the decrease
So you find 100% − 24% = 76%
76% = 0.76
then £2680 × 0.76 = £2036.80

Example

Jo buys a motorbike for £2680.
She sells it for 24% less than this. How much does she get?

Step 1   24% = 0.24   then   £2680 × 0.24 = £643.20

Step 2   Amount at start − decrease = final amount
             £2680   − £643.20 = £2036.80

Jo has made a loss on this bike. You may be asked to find the loss in a question. This will be the decrease.

T E S T   Y O U R S E L F

1 Write each of these as a percentage:

   a $\frac{22}{100}$ **b** $\frac{30}{100}$ **c** $\frac{3}{100}$ **d** $\frac{99}{100}$

2 Write these percentages as fractions out of 100:

   a 40   **b** 4   **c** 88   **d** 47

3 Find each of these:

   a 20% of £400   **b** 9% of £360

4 Find the new amounts after these changes:

   a a 30% increase on £900
   b a 24% profit on £4080
   c a 36% loss on £2150

☐ VAT

> VAT is charged at 17.5%
>
> To find the VAT on an amount you can split it up.
> 17.5% is 10% + 5% + 2.5%
>
> Notice that 2.5% is half of 5% and 5% is half of 10%
>
> so to find VAT   set it out like this:
>
> (1) Find 10% of an amount   10% = ...
>
> (2) Halve this amount to find 5%   5%   = ...
>
> (3) Halve this amount to find 2.5% 2.5% = ...
>
> (4) Add it all together   so 17.5% = _____

Example

A garage bill is £80 + VAT.

a Find the VAT.
b Find the total amount to pay.

a (1) 10% of £80 = $\frac{1}{10}$ of £80 = 80 ÷ 10 = £8

   (2) 5% of £80   = $\frac{1}{2}$ of £8 = 8 ÷ 2   = £4

   (3) 2.5% of £80 = $\frac{1}{2}$ of £4 =   4 ÷ 2   = £2

   (4) Add it all together   so 17.5% = £14

b £80 + £14 = £94

☐ Tax

> Your **tax allowance** is the money you earn before
> paying tax.
>
> Your **taxable income** = your **earnings** – your **tax
> allowance**.
>
> **Income tax** is at 3 rates: 10%, 22% and 40%

Example

Tim earns £5800 a year. His tax allowance is £4500.
He pays tax at the 10% rate.
a What is his taxable income?
b How much tax does he pay each month?

a His taxable income is £5800 – £4500 = £1300
b His taxable income is taxed at 10%.

10% = 0.1

So the tax he pays each year is = 0.1 × £1300 = £130.
Then he pays £130 ÷ 12 = £10.83 tax each month.

Notes

VAT is Value Added Tax.

To find 10%, divide by 10.

You might prefer to do 10% = $\frac{1}{10}$

Then $\frac{1}{10}$ of £80 = £80 ÷ 10 = £8

With a calculator this is a lot easier!

17.5% = 17.5 ÷ 100 = 0.175

then

Earnings are the amount you are paid for
the work you do.

Earnings are usually paid as either wages or
as a salary.

Wages are usually paid weekly.

A salary is usually paid monthly.

You may prefer to use fractions.

10% = $\frac{1}{10}$ so divide by 10

$\frac{1}{10}$ of £1300 = $10\overline{)1300}$ = £130

Expressing one number as a percentage of another

> You have already seen that 7 out of 100 = $\frac{7}{100}$ = 7%
>
> To change numbers to percentages you make them out of 100. With some numbers you can use equivalent fractions.

Example

Change a score of 40 out of 50 to a percentage.

You can write this as a fraction $\frac{40}{50}$

Then you can make it equivalent to a fraction out of 100.

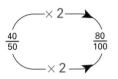 so 40 out of 50 = 80%

See also ▷ **Linking fractions** page 20

> To express one number as a percentage of another number sometimes you cannot use equivalent fractions.
>
> Then you need to use these steps:
> (1) Divide the first number by the second one.
> (2) Multiply by 100.

Examples

Find **a** 38 as a percentage of 40
  b 35 kg as a percentage of 168 kg
  c 5 goals as a percentage of 16 shots

a 38 ÷ 40 = 0.95 then 0.95 × 100 = 95%
b 35 ÷ 168 = 0.2083... then 0.2083... × 100 = 20.1% (1 d.p.)
c 5 ÷ 16 = 0.3125 then 0.3125 × 100 = 31.25%

Notes

To express means to write

This method is particularly useful where the bottom number in the fraction is one of the factors of 100. These are:

1, 2, 4, 5, 10, 20, 25, 50, 100

This is when you cannot multiply the bottom number in a fraction to make 100.

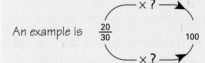

An example is $\frac{20}{30}$ ⟶ 100

You can use this method to work out a percentage change, percentage profit or percentage loss.

Percentage change = $\dfrac{\text{change}}{\text{starting value}}$ × 100

Percentage profit = $\dfrac{\text{profit}}{\text{starting value}}$ × 100

Percentage loss = $\dfrac{\text{loss}}{\text{starting value}}$ × 100

You might be asked to give the last answer to 1 decimal place. If so it would be 31.3%.

TEST YOURSELF

1 Find the VAT on these amounts:

  a £100 **b** £60 **c** £250

  d £32 **e** £4500 **f** £965

2 Pippa earns £8960 per year. Her tax allowance is £4200. Find:

  a her taxable income

  b the tax she pays per month if she pays tax at 10%

3 Write these as percentages:

  a 10 out of 50 **b** 16 out of 50 **c** $\frac{8}{50}$

  d 20 out of 20 **e** 17 out of 20 **f** $\frac{4}{24}$

4 Find the first number as a percentage of the second:

  a 12, 30 **b** 15, 40 **c** 45, 360

  d 25, 75 **e** 48, 1760 **f** 25, 96

Linking fractions, decimals and percentages

☐ Changing fractions to decimals

> The line in a fraction means divide
>
> So you can read $\frac{3}{4}$ as 3 divided by 4.
>
> If you do this, you get a decimal
> $$4\overline{\smash{\big)}\,3\,.\,{}^{3}0^{2}0}\quad\begin{array}{c}0\,.\,7\,5\end{array}$$

Examples

Change to a decimal: **a** $\frac{9}{20}$ **b** $\frac{5}{8}$

a $9 \div 20 = 20\overline{\smash{\big)}\,9\,.\,{}^{9}0\ {}^{10}0}\quad\begin{array}{c}0\,.\,4\;5\end{array}$ **b** $8\overline{\smash{\big)}\,5\,.\,{}^{5}0\ {}^{2}0\ {}^{4}0}\quad\begin{array}{c}0\,.\,6\;2\;5\end{array}$

☐ Changing decimals to percentages

> To change a decimal to a percentage, multiply by 100.

Examples

Change to a percentage: **a** 0.27   **b** 0.04

a $0.27 = 0.27 \times 100\% = 27\%$

b $0.04 = 0.04 \times 100\% = 4\%$

| See also ⇒ | **Multiplying by 10, 100 or 1000** page 3

☐ Changing fractions to percentages

> To do this you just need to combine the last two topics!
>
> (1) Change the fraction to a decimal.
> (2) Change the decimal to a percentage.

Examples

Change to a percentage: **a** $\frac{7}{40}$ **b** $\frac{21}{26}$

a *Step 1* $7 \div 40 = 0.175$
   Step 2 $0.175 \times 100 = 17.5\%$

b *Step 1* $21 \div 26 = 0.8076...$
   Step 2 $0.8076... \times 100 = 80.76\% = 80.8\%$ (to 1 d.p.)

Notes

You can do these on a calculator like this:

| 9 | ÷ | 2 | 0 | = | 0.45 |

| 5 | ÷ | 8 | = | 0.625 |

This is because 100% = 1 whole one
so 1% $= 1 \div 100 = 0.01$
and 100% $= 0.01 \times 100 = 1$

To multiply by 100 move 2 columns left:

H	T	U	t	h
		0.	2	7
	2	7		

H	T	U	t	h
		0	0	4
	4			

You may notice that $\frac{7}{40}$ is the rate of VAT given as a fraction!

TEST YOURSELF

1 Change each of these to decimals:

   a $\frac{3}{5}$ **b** $\frac{1}{4}$ **c** $\frac{2}{3}$ **d** $\frac{3}{8}$

2 Change: **a** 0.09 **b** 0.76 to percentages.

3 Change each of these to percentages:

   a $\frac{2}{5}$ **b** $\frac{3}{4}$ **c** $\frac{7}{8}$ **d** $\frac{5}{7}$

☐ Changing decimals to fractions

For this you need to remember place value.
You also need to be able to cancel down.

H	T	U	tenths	hundredths	thousandths
		0 .	4		
		0 .	3	2	
		0 .	0	0	7

The 4 here is under the tenths column.

So $0.4 = \frac{4}{10}$ then cancelling down gives $\frac{2}{5}$.

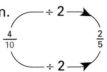

See also ▷ **Place value** page 2

The 2 is under the hundredths column.
So you have to make a fraction over 100.

The fraction is $\frac{32}{100}$ then cancelling down gives $\frac{8}{25}$.

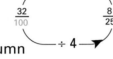

The 7 is under the thousandths column so the fraction is $\frac{7}{1000}$

The further you go to the right with place value, the less the numbers are.

The further you go to the left with place value, the greater the numbers are.

☐ Changing percentages to decimals

The rule here is to divide by 100.
So 27% as a decimal = 27 ÷ 100 = 0.27.

This is because 100% = 1 whole one

so   1%   = 1 ÷ 100 = 0.01

☐ Changing percentages to fractions

Per cent means out of 100 so put the percentage over 100.

Then cancel down if you can.

To divide by 100 move 2 columns right

H	T	U	. t	h
	2	7		
		0	2	7

Examples

Change to a fraction: **a** 77%   **b** 45%

a $77\% = \frac{77}{100}$

b $45\% = \frac{45}{100} = \frac{9}{20}$ then

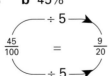

No cancelling is possible in part **a**.

TEST YOURSELF

1 Change each of these to a fraction:

  a 0.3   **b** 0.7   **c** 0.01   **d** 0.08
  e 0.47   **f** 0.75   **g** 0.66   **h** 0.008

2 Change each of these to a decimal:

  a 25%   **b** 70%   **c** 7%   **d** 77%

3 Change each of these to a fraction:

  a 25%   **b** 40%   **c** 65%   **d** 24%

4 Match any cards that show the same amount

| 0.42 | 0.84 | $\frac{21}{50}$ | $2\frac{1}{10}$ | 42% | 21% | $\frac{21}{25}$ |

Ratio

☐ Ratio

Look at these 2 piles of textbooks

The first pile is three times the height of the second one.
Their heights are in the ratio 3 : 1.
The ratio of the numbers of books = 6 : 2
but you can divide both sides of the ratio by 2
so

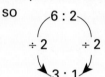

Examples

Look at each of these pairs of pictures.
For each one write down the ratio of their numbers.

a   **b**

a The ratio is   8 : 2
    which cancels to   4 : 1

b The ratio is   10 : 8
    which cancels to   5 : 4

☐ Sharing out using ratio

Look at these cans. Emma and Matt share them in the ratio 3 : 2. How many does each get?

To do this question you need to find the number of shares.

There are 3 + 2 shares = 5 shares.

There are 20 cans, so each share = 20 ÷ 5 = 4 cans.

So Martha gets 3 × 4 = 12 cans and Vicky gets
2 × 4 = 8 cans.

Example

Heather shares £240 between her 3 sons, Ben, Den and Len in the ratio 1 : 2 : 5. How much does each son receive?

Number of shares = 1 + 2 + 5 = 8
Each share   = 240 ÷ 8 = £30.

So Ben gets 1 × 30 = £30   Den gets 2 × 30 = £60
                               and Len gets 5 × 30 = £150.

Notes

Ratio is used to compare quantities.

If the piles were reversed they would be in the ratio 1 : 3.

This is very like cancelling with fractions.

This means that for every 3 cans Emma has, Matt has 2.

Every time Emma gets 3 cans Matt gets 2, so that 5 cans are given out altogether.

You can check if an answer is correct by adding all the amounts at the end.

Here £30 + £60 + £150 = £240.

This agrees with the amount at the start so the answers must be correct.

☐ Value for money

Suppose you need to compare the value for money of two items.

To do this you work out the price for a fixed amount.

Example

Soup costs 56 p for a 400 g can and 84 p for a 700 g can. Which is better value?

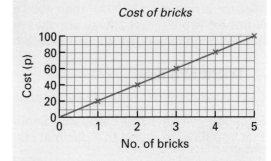

You need to work out how much it is for each 100 g of soup.

400 g can: 56 p ÷ 4 = 14 p per 100 g

700 g can: 84 p ÷ 7 = 12 p per 100 g

The 700 g can is better value. You pay less per 100 g.

☐ Direct proportion

Suppose bricks cost 20 p each. So 1 brick costs 20 p.

Then 2 bricks cost 40 p and 3 bricks cost 60 p.

In this situation the price increases at the same rate.

This is called **direct proportion**.

Example

Here are the prices of some stamps.
Fill in the gaps in this table marked with letters.

Amount	1	2	5	18	c
Cost	27 p	54 p	a	b	£5.94

a 5 stamps will cost 5 times as much as 1 stamp
5 × 27 = £1.35

b 18 stamps will cost 18 times as much as 1 stamp
18 × 27 = £4.86

c Divide the total cost by the cost for 1 stamp
594 ÷ 27 = 22

Notes

A question might give you the masses of some cans as 420 g and 760 g. To compare them you would need to find the cost per 10 g. You would divide the 420 g price by 42 and the 760 g price by 76.

Another question might give you the masses of some cans as 456 g and 847 g. Here it is best to find the amount you get per penny.

If the 456 g cost 38 p and the 847 g cost 77 p, then the masses per penny would be:
456 ÷ 38 = 12 g per penny.
847 ÷ 77 = 11 g per penny.
Here the 456 g can is better value as you get more grams for each penny.

If you plotted a graph of the cost of the bricks it would be a straight line.

Cost of bricks

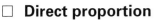

Make sure you are dividing with both costs in the same units. Here it is best to change everything into pence.

TEST YOURSELF

1 A large packet of grass seed has a mass of 10 kg. A smaller packet has a mass of 2 kg. What is the ratio of the big bag to the small bag?

2 A cereal is made by mixing oats, wheat and maize in the ratio 5 : 2 : 1. What mass of wheat is needed to make 24 kg of cereal?

3 Which packet of crisps below is the best value:
a 30 g packet for 36 p or
a 180 g packet for £1.98?

4 Fill in the gaps marked with letters in this table.

Number of rolls	1	2	4	8	c
Cost	16 p	32 p	a	b	£4.48

Rounding

☐ Rounding numbers to the nearest 10, 100, 1000

Examples

1 Round the mass 24 g to the nearest 10 g

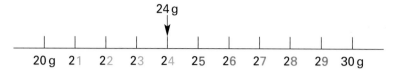

24 g is nearer to 20 g than 30 g.
Numbers less than halfway are always rounded down.
It is rounded to 20 g to the nearest 10 g.

2 Round the length 450 m to the nearest 100 m

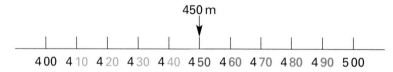

450 m is halfway between 400 m and 500 m.
Numbers that are halfway are always rounded up.
It is 500 m to the nearest 100 m.

3 Round the area 4640 m² to the nearest 1000 m².

4640 m² is nearer to 5000 m² than 4000 m².
Numbers more than halfway are always rounded up.
It is rounded to 5000 m² to the nearest 1000 m².

☐ Decimal places

Calculator displays often give you lots of decimal places.

Suppose you have this calculator display
that you have to round to 1 decimal place. *56.48164379*

Draw a line after 1 d.p.   5 6 . 4 | 8

Put your finger over the numbers after the 8.
The 8 is 5 or more so you round up.
So the answer is 56.5 to 1 decimal place.

Notes

The further you go to the left on a number line, the less the numbers are.

The further you go to the right on a number line, the greater the numbers are.

25 is exactly halfway between 20 and 30. The blue numbers are less than halfway. The green numbers are more than halfway.

Whatever the units, the same rules of rounding apply.

Use the same rules of rounding for 2 or more decimal places. So here this display would be: 56.48 to 2 decimal places,
56.482 to 3 decimal places,
56.4816 to 4 decimal places.

Unit 15 pages 353–4

TEST YOURSELF

1 Round these numbers to the nearest 10:

    a 42   **b** 58   **c** 75
    d 7   **e** 55   **f** 98

2 Round these numbers to the nearest 100:

    a 720   **b** 750   **c** 785
    d 191   **e** 800   **f** 998

3 Round these numbers to the nearest 1000:

    a 2050   **b** 3500   **c** 5495

4 Round these lengths to 1 decimal place:

    a 12.65 cm   **b** 84.15 m   **c** 17.37902 km

5 Round these masses to 2 decimal places:

    a 68.415 g   **b** 4.373 t   **c** 0.094 099 kg

Significant figures

In any number the first **significant figure** is the first digit which isn't a 0. For most numbers this is the first digit.

The first significant figure is the digit in red:

32.9   4096   9.01   0.78   0.0032

Rounding to any number of significant figures

To do this you:

- look at the first unwanted digit
- if it is 5, 6, 7, 8, or 9, add one on to the digit you keep
- if it is 0, 1, 2, 3 or 4 ignore it
- keep the number about the right size.

Examples

Round these numbers:

a 45 to 1 s.f.   **b** 35 684 to 2 s.f.   **c** 0.722 4 to 3 s.f.

a 45 is 50 to 1 s.f.
It is <u>not</u> 5!

40 41 42 43 44 45 46 47 48 49 50

b 35 684 is 36 000 to 2 s.f. It is not 36.

c 0.722 4 is 0.722 to 3 s.f.

Estimating

To do this you round each number to 1 significant figure.

Examples

Estimate: **a** 8.7 × 6.3   **b** 267 × 64   **c** 4096 ÷ 769

a 8.7 × 6.3 ≈ 9 × 6 = 54   (calc. 54.81)
b 267 × 64 ≈ 300 × 60 = 18 000   (calc. 17 088)
c 4096 ÷ 769 ≈ 4000 ÷ 800 = 40 ÷ 8 = 5   (calc. 5.3 to 1 d.p.)

Notes

Significant figures are normally abbreviated to s.f.

This is one of the most common mistakes when finding significant figures.

35 684 could be a typical premier league football attendance. But it is obvious that there would be roughly 36 000 at the game not 36.

≈ means 'roughly' or 'approximately equal to'.

The calculated answer is shown in brackets.

Unit 13 pages 309–310

TEST YOURSELF

1 Write down the first significant figure in each of these numbers:

   a 4276   **b** 7.6   **c** 0.030 405

2 Round each of these numbers to 1 s.f.:

   a 22   **b** 6.3   **c** 49
   d 586   **e** 9187   **f** 0.275

3 Round these numbers:

   a 2.3492 to 2 s.f.   **b** 0.069 91 to 3 s.f.
   c 48.926 to 3 s.f.   **d** 54 678 to 3 s.f.

4 Work these out. Do an estimate for each one.

   a 7.6 × 4.2   **b** 283 ÷ 39   **c** 7.6 + 9.2
   d 8.91 − 2.63   **e** 48 × 674   **f** 8352 ÷ 187

Changing currencies

☐ Exchange rate

> You can find how much £1 is worth in foreign currency by looking at the **exchange rate**.

Example

Eddie goes to Belgium. The exchange rate is 60 francs to £1. He changed £15 into francs (F). How much did he receive?

Every £1 he has is worth 60 francs.
So he receives 15 × 60 = 900 F.

> You can use an exchange rate to work out the cost of goods.
>
> In Germany a snowboard costs 126 marks (DM)
> The exchange rate is £1 = 2.86 DM.
>
> As every 2.86 marks is worth £1, you need to find how many lots of 2.86 there are in 126.
> This is 126 ÷ 2.86 = 44.055 94...
>
> So the price is £44.06 to the nearest penny.

☐ Conversion graphs

You use these to change from one currency to another.
To change $3 to yen, follow the red line to give 350 Y.
To change 700 yen to $, follow the green line to give $6.

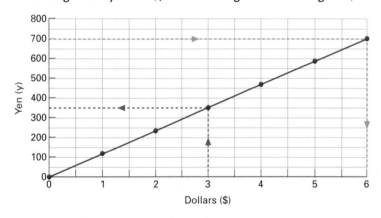

Notes

Every currency has its own exchange rate. You are not expected to remember them! Several countries have Francs as their currency. These include France, Belgium and Switzerland but their exchange rates are all different.

You could do this by long multiplication:

```
      60
    × 15
   ─────
     300        60 × 5
     600        60 × 10
   ─────
     900
```

Exchange rates change from day to day. You can find an up-to-date list in most newspapers and banks.

You round 44.055 94... like this:

44.05|5 ⬭⑴ ⑴

The 5 after the line rounds the 5 before the line up to 6.
Whatever the units, the same rules of rounding apply.

TEST YOURSELF

1 The exchange rate for US dollars is £1 = $1.58.

Change these amounts into US dollars:
a £10   **b** £22   **c** £760

Change these amounts into pounds:
d $316   **e** $71.10   **f** $193.55

2 In the chart to the right:

a How many krona are 3 rand worth?
b How many rand are 6 krona worth?

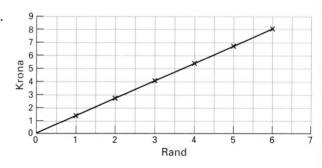

BODMAS

☐ **BODMAS**

Calculators always work calculations out in a special order.

When you work sums out, you need to use the same order.

First do   then   next do   and   before you do

B	O	D	M	A	S
R	P W	I	U	D	U
A	E	V	L	D	B
C	R	I	T		T
K	S	D	I		R
E		E	P		A
T			L		C
S			Y		T

P
B R A C K E T S
O W E R S
D I V I D E
M U L T I P L Y
A D D
S U B T R A C T

Examples

Work these out: **a** $7 + 8 \times 3$ **b** $14 - 8 \div 2$

a $7 + 8 \times 3$ B O D **M** A S   Do $\times$ before $+$

   $= 7 + 24 = 31$

b $14 - 8 \div 2$ B O **D** M A S   Do $\div$ before $-$

   $= 14 - 4 = 10$

You always do brackets first.

Example

Work out: $4 \times (20 - 15)$

     $4 \times (20 - 15)$ B O D **M** A S   Do ( ) before $\times$

   $= 4 \times 5 = 20$

You always do any powers (squaring, cubing, etc.) straight after any brackets.

Examples

Work these out: **a** $4 \times 5^2 - 3$ **b** $\dfrac{73 - 5^2}{2^3 \times \sqrt{9}}$

a $4 \times 5^2 - 3$ B **O** D **M** A **S**   Do p**O**wers then $\times$ then $-$

   $= 4 \times 25 - 3 = 100 - 3 = 97$

b $(73 - 5^2) \div (2^3 \times \sqrt{9})$ Inside the ( ) do p**O**wers first.

   $= (73 - 25) \div (8 \times 3)$ Now finish what is in each ( ).

   $= 48 \div 24 = 2$ Do ( ) before $\div$

Notes

Order is very important when you do sums. If it wasn't, many sums would have more than one answer.

BODMAS helps you to remember the order to use.

When two things have equal importance, like multiply and divide, you should *work from left to right*.

So $12 \div 4 \times 3$ gives $3 \times 3 = 9$,
not $12 \div 12 = 1$.

If you had to do
$(18 - 6) \div (2 \times 3)$
Then you could do both pairs of brackets at the same time to give
$12 \div 6 = 2$

In part **b** below $\dfrac{73 - 5^2}{2^3 \times \sqrt{9}}$ the fraction line

acts like brackets on the top and bottom.

You could also use a calculator here.

Do   [5] [x^2]   to square 5

Both brackets can be done at the same time, but you must do what is *in* them first.

Do   [2] [x^y] [3]   to cube 2.

Do   [√] [9]   to take the square root of 9.

☐ Powers

> It is easier to write $2 + 2 + 2 + 2$ as 4×2.
>
> You can also write $2 \times 2 \times 2 \times 2$ more easily as 2^4.
>
> This means 2 to the power of 4 and it has the value 16.

Examples

1 Work out: **a** 6^3 **b** $2^2 \times 5^3$

   a 6^3 means 3 lots of 6 multiplied together, so

$$6^3 = \underline{6 \times 6} \times 6$$
$$= \underline{36 \times 6}$$
$$= 216$$

   b $2^2 \times 5^3 = \underline{2 \times 2} \quad \times \quad \underline{5 \times 5 \times 5}$
$$= \quad 4 \quad \times \quad \underline{25 \times 5}$$
$$= \quad 4 \quad \times \quad 125 \quad = \quad 500$$

2 Write each of these using powers.

   a $4 \times 4 \times 4 \times 4 \times 4$ **b** $7 \times 7 \times 7 \times 7 \times 5 \times 5$

   a $4 \times 4 \times 4 \times 4 \times 4 = 4^5$ **b** $7 \times 7 \times 7 \times 7 \times 5 \times 5 = 7^4 \times 5^2$

☐ Squaring and cubing

> The square of a number is the number to the power of 2.
> The cube   of a number is the number to the power of 3.

See also ⟩ **Squares and square roots** page 10

☐ Using a power key on a calculator

> You can use the y^x key or x^y key to work out any power.
>
> To find 2^6 key in   or
>
>   2 x^y 6
>
> to get 64.

Notes

You have 4 lots of 2 added together.

You have 4 lots of 2 multiplied together. Without a calculator you can work it out like this:

$$2 \times 2 \times 2 \times 2$$
$$= \quad 4 \quad \times 2 \times 2$$
$$= \quad\quad 8 \quad \times 2$$
$$= \quad\quad\quad 16$$

A common mistake is to write 6^3 is 18. Can you think why?
It is because you might think 6^3 is 3 lots of 6, but 6^3 is actually 36 lots of 6.

This is why it is a good idea to only multiply two numbers together at one go, then as soon as you get $6 \times 6 = 36$ you will realise that 6^3 cannot be 18.

Just count how many of each number you have got to find the power.

You cannot write $7^4 \times 5^2$ as one power.

You can say 3 squared or the square of 3.

You can say 7 cubed or the cube of 7.

TEST YOURSELF

1 Work these out:

   a $4 \times 3 + 2$ **b** $9 - 2 + 7$ **c** $12 - 8 \div 2$
   d $6 \div 3 \times 2$ **e** $24 - 8 \div 4$ **f** $3 + 2 \times 4 - 3$

2 Work these out. Show all your working.

   a $3 + 5^2$ **b** $20 - 4^2$ **c** $5^2 - 3^3$
   d $32 \times (3^5 - 241)$ **e** $\dfrac{27 - 5^2 + 8}{\sqrt{16} \times 2\frac{1}{2}}$

3 Work these out. Show all your working.

   a 6^2 **b** 5^3 **c** 4^4
   d $2^2 \times 4^3$ **e** $5^4 \times 3^2$ **f** $7^2 \times 8^2$

4 Write each of these using powers:

   a $3 \times 3 \times 3 \times 3$ **b** $9 \times 9 \times 9 \times 2 \times 2$

5 Use a calculator to work these out:

   a 10^5 **b** $2^7 \times 3^4$ **c** $8^5 \div 2^6$

Standard form

You can use **standard form** to write very large numbers.

A number in standard form has two parts, a number from 1 up to 9.9... multiplied by 10 to a power.

A number like 20 000 can be written in standard form.

It is 2×10^4.

You can work out the value of a number in standard form if you use what you already know about powers.

Example

Work out the value of 6.3×10^3

Th	H	T	U	t	6.3
←	←	←	6	. 3	× 1000
6	3	0	0		= 6 300

☐ Standard form on calculator displays

Very large numbers get changed on calculator displays.

They use **standard form** to write very large numbers.

Some new calculators display 2.3×10^9 like this $2.3^{\times 10^{09}}$

Others still display 2.3×10^9 like this 2.3^{09}

Example

Write these displays in standard form: **a** $9.2^{\times 10^{12}}$ **b** 5.26^{17}

a $9.2^{\times 10^{12}} = 9.2 \times 10^{12}$ **b** $5.26^{17} = 5.26 \times 10^{17}$

☐ Using the EXP or EE key on a calculator

To enter 4.62×10^7 just key in **4** **.** **6** **2** **EXP** **7**

Example

Work out $(4 \times 10^8) \times (7.1 \times 10^9)$. Answer in standard form.

Key in **4** **EXP** **8** **×** **7** **.** **1** **EXP** **9** **=** 2.84×10^{18}

Notes

Notes

Numbers can be written in standard form like this:

- put an arrow after the first digit,
- count the rest of the digits to the decimal point, this is the power of 10.

so $\quad 2\ 0\ 0\ 0\ 0 = 2 \times 10^4$

and $\quad 6\ 3\ 0\ 0 = 6.3 \times 10^3$

$10^3 = 10 \times 10 \times 10 = 1000$

You need to be sure you can write down these displays in standard form. You must make sure you put the ×10 part in.

Some calculators have an **EE** key or an **Exp** key instead of an **EXP** key. If yours has, use it in exactly the same way as shown for the **EXP** key.

TEST YOURSELF

1 Write these calculator displays in standard form.

a $5^{\times 10^{08}}$ **b** $9.6^{\times 10^{17}}$ **c** $6.093^{\times 10^{12}}$
d 6^{09} **e** 1.48^{22} **f** 2.007^{18}

2 Use a calculator to work these out.
Give your answers in standard form.

a $1\,000\,000 \times 20\,000$ **b** $400\,000 \times 600\,000$
c $360\,000 \times 420\,000$ **d** $12\,500\,000 \times 72\,000$

3 Use a calculator to work these out.
Give your answers in standard form.

a $(1.2 \times 10^2) \times (4 \times 10^9)$
b $(4.9 \times 10^6) \times (2.2 \times 10^{11})$
c $(7.3 \times 10^{14}) \times (9 \times 10^{14})$
d $(9.6 \times 10^{21}) \div (4.8 \times 10^{20})$
e $(6.3 \times 10^{12}) \div (2.1 \times 10^9)$
f $(6.02 \times 10^{23}) \div 236$

Practice questions

1 a i A small bag of potatoes weighs 5 kg.
A large bag of potatoes weighs 60% more than a small bag.
What is the weight of a large bag of potatoes? *(2)*

ii The ratio of the price of a small bag of potatoes to the price of a large
bag of potatoes is 3 : 4.
A small bag costs 96 pence.
What is the price of a large bag? *(3)*

b Carrots are sold in bags and sacks.
Bags of carrots weigh 3 kg and cost 72 pence.
Sacks of carrots weigh 14 kg and cost £2.66.
How much, per kilogram, is saved by buying sacks of carrots instead of
buying bags of carrots? *(3)*

SEG, 1999, Paper 12

2 Do not use a calculator to answer this question.
Alun has a part-time job.
He is paid £18 each day he works.
In 1998 he worked 148 days.

a Estimate Alun's total pay for 1998.
Write down your calculation and answer. *(3)*

b Work out exactly how much Alun was paid in 1998.
Show all your working. *(3)*

NEAB, 1999, Paper 2

3 A formula to estimate the number of rolls of wallpaper, *R*, for a room is

$$R = \frac{ph}{5}$$ where *p* is the perimeter of the room in metres
and *h* is the height of the room in metres.

The perimeter of Carol's bedroom is 15.5 m and it is 2.25 m high.
How many rolls of wallpaper will she have to buy? *(3)*

NEAB, 1999, Paper 2

2 Algebra

- [ ] **Formulas**
- [ ] **Patterns**
- [ ] **Equations**
- [ ] **Graphs**

Formulas

☐ Formulas using words

> A formula is a set of instructions.
>
> It tells you how to work something out.
>
> This formula tells you how to work out the cost in pounds of hiring a carpet cleaner.
>
> Cost = 5 + 3 × number of days

Example

Find out the cost of hiring a carpet cleaner for 6 days.

Cost = 5 + 3 × 6
       = 5 + 18
       = 23

The cost is £23.

☐ Working backwards using formulas

Example

John paid £17. How many days did he hire the cleaner for?

17 = 5 + 3 × number of days
12 = 3 × number of days
 4 = number of days

☐ Formulas using letters

> Formulas can be written using letters instead of words.
>
> The perimeter P of a rectangle is given by
>
> $P = 2(l + w)$
>
> l is the length of the rectangle and w is the width.

Example

Use the formula to find the perimeter of this rectangle.

$P = 2(l + w)$
   $= 2(11 + 5)$
   $= 2 \times 16$
   $= 32$

The perimeter is 32 cm.

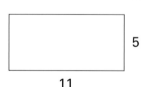

☐ Writing your own formulas

> Pick out the important words and numbers.
> Choose letters to stand for the important words.

Example

The cost of hiring a car is £15 plus £20 for each day.
Write a formula for the cost of hiring the car.

    $C = 15 + 20d$

Notes

A formula does not contain units.

Remember to multiply first then add 5.
The number of days is replaced by 6.

Always write down the answer.

Don't forget the units.

The cost is 17.
Take 5 from each side.
Divide each side by 3.

Work out the bracket first – use BODMAS.
Multiply the number inside the bracket by the 2.

Remember not to include units like cm or £ in your formula.

Use C for the cost and d for the number of days. 20d means 20 × d.

Unit 5 pages 115–120

☐ Using formulas

Example

Find the value of $7a - 3b$ when $a = 6$ and $b = 2$.
$$7a - 3b = 7 \times 6 - 3 \times 2$$
$$= 42 - 6$$
$$= 36$$

Substitute means replace a letter with a number.

☐ Substituting decimals

You can substitute decimals into a formula.

Example

$y = 7x + 4$
Find the value of y when $x = 3.2$
$$y = 7 \times 3.2 + 4$$
$$= 22.4 + 4$$
$$= 26.4$$

☐ Substituting fractions

You can substitute fractions into a formula.

Example

$P = 2(5l + w)$
Find the value of P when $l = \frac{1}{2}$ and $w = \frac{1}{4}$.
$$P = 2\left(5 \times \frac{1}{2} + \frac{1}{4}\right)$$
$$= 2 \times 2\frac{3}{4}$$
$$= 5\frac{1}{2}$$

☐ Formulas with powers

Example

$V = 3p^2 - 4t$
Find V when $p = 5$ and $t = 3\frac{1}{4}$.
$$V = 3 \times 5^2 - 4 \times 3\frac{1}{4}$$
$$= 3 \times 25 - 13$$
$$= 62$$

Notes

Replace a by the number 6 and b by 2.
Use the rules of BODMAS: so $\times$ before $-$

x is replaced by 3.2

Use the $a^{b/c}$ key on your calculator to key in fractions:

$\frac{1}{2}$ is   1 $a^{b/c}$ 2

Work out the bracket first, use BODMAS.
Multiply the number inside the bracket by the 2 in front of the bracket.

Remember for powers like 7^3 the 3 tells you how many 7s are multiplied together so $7^3 = 7 \times 7 \times 7$.

p^2 means $p \times p$ $3p^2$ means $3 \times p \times p$

5^2 means 5×5 3×5^2 means $3 \times 5 \times 5$

BODMAS: $\times$ then $-$

Unit 13 pages 311–315

TEST YOURSELF

1   The rule for changing miles into kilometres is:
    multiply the number of miles by 8 and divide by 5. Use the formula to change 25 miles into kilometres.

2   **a** Lisa's wage W is made up of £8 plus £5 for each skirt she makes. Write a formula for W if Lisa makes n skirts.
    b Lisa makes 12 skirts. Find her wage.

3   $v = u + at$
    Find v when $u = 2.5$, $a = 3.6$ and $t = 8$.

4   $R = 3p - 8$
    a Find R when $p = 4$.
    b Find p when $R = 22$.

5   $y = 2x^3$
    Find y when $x = 5$.

Patterns

☐ Number sequences

A number sequence is a list of numbers that follow a rule.

Each number is called a term.

The first number is the 1st term, the second number is the 2nd term, the third number is the 3rd term and so on.

☐ Formula for a sequence of numbers

You can write a formula for a number sequence.

The multiples of 2 form a sequence 2 4 6 8 10 ...

The formula for the *n*th term of the sequence is 2*n* where *n* is the term number. You can work out any term using this formula.

To find the 25th term substitute 25 for *n*

The 25th term = $2 \times 25 = 50$

The multiples of 3 have the formula   3*n*

The multiples of 4 have the formula   4*n*

The multiples of 5 have the formula   5*n*

and so on.

Example

Look at the sequence: 6 12 18 24 30 ......

a Write down a formula for the sequence.

b Find the 50th term in the sequence.

a

The rule is 'add 6'.
So the formula is 6*n*.

b The 50th term = $6 \times 50 = 300$

Always find what has been added each time.

Substitute 50 for *n*.

TEST YOURSELF

Find each of these number sequences

    a Write down the formula

    b Find the 20th term

1   10 20 30 40 50 ...

2   7 14 21 28 35 ...

3   9 18 27 36 45 ...

4 a By drawing a diagram, find the formula for the number sequence:

    $\frac{1}{2}$ 1 $1\frac{1}{2}$ 2 $2\frac{1}{2}$ ...

  b Find the 10th number in the sequence

  c Find the 50th number in the sequence

☐ Formulas with two parts

Notes

Look at this sequence:

  5 7 9 11 13 ...

Find the differences between terms.

The rule is add 2, but the sequence is not the multiples of 2.

Write the terms of $2n$ underneath the sequence.

The multiples of 2 start with 2
The multiples of 3 start with 3
and so on.

Sequence	5	7	9	11	13
Formula $2n$	2	4	6	8	10

You need to add 3 to every term of $2n$ to get to the sequence.

The formula is $2n + 3$.

Check your formula works by finding a term you already know.
        3rd term = 2 × 3 + 3 = 9 ✓

Example

Find the formula for this sequence: 3 8 13 18 23 ...

Sequence	3	8	13	18	23
Formula $2n$	5	10	15	20	25

You have to subtract 2 to get from $5n$ to the sequence.
The formula is $5n - 2$.

The difference is 5 so use 5n.
Look for what you have to do to get to the sequence.

☐ Using the formula for a sequence

You can use the formula for a sequence to work out the value of any term.

Example

The formula for the nth term of a sequence is $6n + 5$

a Find the first three terms.

b Find the 46th term.

c Which term has the value 143?

Unit 10 pages 238–241

a The 1st term $= 6 \times 1 + 5 = 6 + 5 = 11$
   The 2nd term $= 6 \times 2 + 5 = 12 + 5 = 17$
   The 3rd term $= 6 \times 3 + 5 = 18 + 5 = 23$

b The 42nd term $= 6 \times 42 + 5 = 252 + 5 = 257$

c $143 = 6n + 5$
   $138 = 6n$
   $23 = n$
   The 23rd term has the value 143.

Substitute 1 for n.
Substitute 2 for n.
Substitute 3 for n.
Substitute 42 for n.

Take 5 from both sides.
Divide both sides by 6.

TEST YOURSELF

1 The formula for the nth term of a sequence is $5n - 4$.

   a Find the first three terms of the sequence.

   b Find the 80th term.

   c Which term has the value 156?

2 Find the formulas for these sequences:

   a 7 10 13 16 19 ...

   b 4 10 16 22 28 ...

   c 13 23 33 43 53 ...

☐ Patterns with shapes

Notes

You can get a number sequence from patterns of shapes.

Example

These patterns are made out of triangles.

a Draw the next pattern.

b Write down the number of triangles in the patterns as a number sequence.

c Find a formula for the sequence.

 Use *n* for the number of triangles.

d Find the number of triangles in the 100th pattern.

a

b The number sequence is: 6 10 14 18

c The pattern goes up in 4s. It is related to 4*n*

Work out the differences.

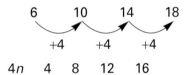

 You have to add 2 to get to the sequence.

 The formula is 4*n* + 2

Check the formula works by using it to find the 4th term: $4 \times 4 + 2 = 18$

d 100th term = $4 \times 100 + 2 = 402$

 There are 402 triangles in the 100th pattern.

Substitute 100 for n.

Unit 10 pages 242–243

TEST YOURSELF

1 These patterns are made with sticks.

a Draw the next pattern.

b Write down the number of sticks as a number sequence.

c Work out the formula for the number of sticks.

d How many sticks will there be in the 12th pattern?

e Which pattern number will have 177 sticks?

2 These patterns are made with counters.

a Draw the next pattern.

b Work out the formula for the number of counters in the *n*th pattern.

c Which pattern has 83 counters?

d How many counters would you need to make pattern 55?

Equations

☐ Solving equations

> When you solve an equation you are trying to work out the value of a letter. To do this you get the letter by itself on one side of the equation.

Example

Solve: **a** $5x - 3 = 17$ **b** $\dfrac{y}{3} + 6 = 15$

a $5x - 3 = 17$
$\quad 5x = 20$
$\quad\;\; x = 4$

b $\dfrac{y}{3} + 8 = 15$
$\qquad \dfrac{y}{3} = 7$
$\qquad\; y = 21$

a Add 3 to both sides.
Divide both sides by 5.

b Take 8 from both sides to get the $\dfrac{y}{3}$ on its own.
Multiply both sides by 3.

☐ Equations with letters on both sides

> You need to change the equation so that the letter is only on one side.
>
> Look to see which side has the larger number of the letter and move all the letters to this side.

Example

Solve: **a** $7t = 3t + 12$ **b** $4x + 20 = 6x$

a $7t = 3t + 12$
$\quad 4t = 12$
$\quad\; t = 3$

b $4x + 20 = 6x$
$\qquad\;\; 20 = 2x$
$\qquad\;\; 10 = x$

a 3t is less than 7t.
Take 3t from both sides.
Divide both sides by 4.

b 4x is less than 6x.
Take 4x from both sides.
Divide both sides by 2.

☐ Equations with letters and numbers on both sides

> Change the equation so that the letter is on one side and the numbers are on the other side.

Unit 15 pages 356–361

Example

Solve: $9a - 14 = 5a + 6$
$\qquad\;\; 4a - 14 = 6$
$\qquad\qquad 4a = 20$
$\qquad\qquad\; a = 5$

5a is less than 9a.
Take 5a from both sides.
Add 14 to both sides.
Divide both sides by 4

TEST YOURSELF

1 Solve these equations:

a $5m + 3 = 18$

b $\dfrac{x}{2} - 7 = 1$

c $19 = 9 + 2h$

2 Solve these equations:

a $8m = 20 + 3m$

b $x + 35 = 6x$

c $24 + 5y = 6y$

d $18 - 2x = x$

☐ Forming equations

Sometimes you have to form the equation before solving it.

Example

The distance travelled by a train is equal to the speed multiplied by the time.

The train travels 225 km in 3 hours.

a Write a formula for the distance, *D*, travelled.

b Use your formula to find the speed of the train.

a $D = S \times T$

b $225 = S \times 3$

$S = \dfrac{225}{3} = 75$ km per hour

Example

These two rectangles have the same area.

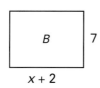

a Write down a formula for the area of each rectangle.

b Write down an equation in terms of *x*.

c Solve your equation to find the area of the rectangles.

a Area of rectangle $A = 3(x + 10)$
Area of rectangle $B = 7(x + 2)$

b $3(x + 10) = 7(x + 2)$

c $3x + 30 = 7x + 14$
$\quad\ 30 = 4x + 14$
$\quad\ 16 = 4x$
$\quad\quad x = 4$

The area of rectangle *A* is $3(4 + 10) = 3 \times 14 = 42$

☐ Collecting terms

To collect terms together they must have exactly the same letters in them.

Example

Simplify these by collecting terms:

a $6p - 2p + p$ **b** $8a + 5ab - 3a + 2ba$

a $6p - 2p = 4p$ and $4p + p = 5p$
so $6p - 2p + p = 5p$

b $8a - 3a = 5a$ and $5ab + 2ba = 7ab$
so $8a + 5ab - 3a + 2ba = 5a + 7ab$

Notes

Replace 'is equal to' by an = sign.
Look out for 'is the same as' or just 'is' sometimes.

Use *S* for speed and *T* for time.
The distance is 225 and the time is 3.

This means the equation involves x terms.

$3 \times (x + 10)$ is written $3(x + 10)$
$3(x + 10)$ means $3 \times x + 3 \times 10$

Put the two areas equal to each other.

Multiply out the brackets.
3x is less than 7x so take 3x from both sides.

Use the area of *B* to check your answer.
It should give the same answer.
$7(4 + 2) = 7 \times 6 = 42$

Unit 18 pages 412–416

All the terms involve just *p* so they can be collected together. *p* means 1*p*.
a is not the same as *ab*.
ba is the same as *ab*.

☐ Collecting terms with powers

In y^4 the power 4 tells you that there are four ys multiplied together

so $y^4 = y \times y \times y \times y$

Terms ab^2 and b^2a are the same.

Terms ab^2 and a^2b are not the same because the 2 has moved letters.

Terms x and x^2 are not the same because one involves a power.

Example

Simplify: $5h + 2h^2 - 2h + 6h^2 - h^2$

$\qquad 5h - 2h = 3h$ and $2h^2 + 6h^2 - h^2 = 7h^2$

$\qquad$ So $\quad 5h + 2h^2 - 2h + 6h^2 - h^2 = 3h + 7h^2$

Collect the h terms, then the h^2 terms.

☐ Multiplying out brackets

You multiply everything inside the bracket by the number outside.

So $\quad 5(d - 3)$ becomes $5 \times d - 5 \times 3 = 5d - 15$

and $\quad 3(2y + 7)$ becomes $3 \times 2y + 3 \times 7 = 6y + 21$

Unit 17 pages 396–400 >

☐ Trial and improvement

You can solve problems and equations by trial and improvement.

Guess an answer. Keep improving your guesses, trying to get closer each time.

Unit 18 pages 431–436 >

TEST YOURSELF

1 The rectangle and the square have the same perimeter.

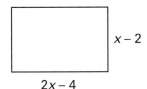

x · x · $x - 2$ · $2x - 4$

  a Write a formula for the perimeter of:

    i the rectangle   **ii** the square.

  b Write down an equation in terms of x.

  c Solve your equation to find the perimeters.

2 Simplify these by collecting terms:

  a $7t + 2t - 5t - t$

  b $6xy + 3y - xy + 2y + 4yx$

  c $4b^2 + b^2 - 3b^2$

  d $7x^2 + 6x - 4x - 3x^2$

3 Multiply out these brackets:

  a $6(y + 2)$ **b** $3(4d - 5)$

  c $4(2m - 1)$ **d** $7(3x - 4y)$

4 Solve these equations by trial and improvement:

  a $x^2 = 1089$ **b** $y^3 = 12\,167$

Graphs

☐ Reading values from graphs

> Before you read values from a graph check the scale on each axis.

Example

The graph shows the value of a £1 investment after a number of years.

Use the graph to find:

a the value after 3 years

b how many years it takes to reach £1.50

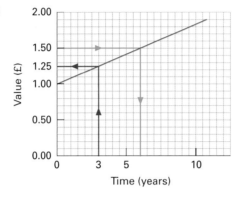

a The value after 3 years is £1.25

b It takes 6 years.

☐ Conversion graphs

> You use a conversion graph to change from one unit to another.

Example

This graph allows you to convert Euros (€) and £s.

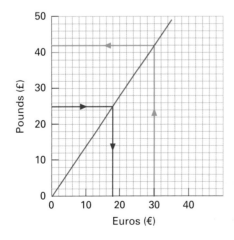

a Convert £25 to Euros   £25 is equivalent to €18.

b Convert €30 to £s.   €30 is equivalent to £42.

Unit 4 pages 88–90

40

Notes

On the time axis 10 squares = 5 years
So 2 squares = 1 year

On the value axis 10 squares = £1
So 1 square = 10p

Follow the blue line to find the value after 3 years.

Follow the green line to find the time it takes to reach a value of £1.50.

Conversion graphs are always straight lines.

On the £ axis 1 square = £2

On the Euro axis 1 square = €2

Follow the blue line to convert £25 to Euros.

Follow the green line to convert €30 to £s.

☐ Travel graphs

> Travel graphs are used to show distance and time.
> They show the distance something has moved
> away from a starting point.

Notes

Time always goes on the horizontal axis.

Example

This graph shows Jim's journey to work.

He walks the first part and then catches a bus.

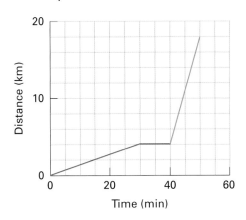

On the time axis 1 square = 5 minutes

On the distance axis 1 square = 2 km

The red line shows the first part of his journey.
He walks 4 km in 30 minutes.

The blue horizontal line shows that he stopped for 10 minutes.

The green line shows the part of the journey he travelled by bus.
Jim travelled 14 km in 10 minutes on the bus.

The green line is steeper than the red line. This is because the bus travelled faster than Jim walked.

The total distance Jim travelled to work is 18 km. His journey took a total time of 50 minutes.

☐ Table of values

Unit 4 pages 91–93

> You can use a formula to draw a table.
>
> If you use the formula $y = 2x - 1$ you will get the following table.
>
> | x | 1 | 2 | 3 | 4 |
> |---|---|---|---|---|
> | y | 1 | 3 | 5 | 7 |

When $x = 1$, $y = 2 \times 1 - 1 = 1$
When $x = 2$, $y = 2 \times 2 - 1 = 3$
When $x = 3$, $y = 2 \times 3 - 1 = 5$
When $x = 4$, $y = 2 \times 4 - 1 = 7$

Example

Jack uses this formula to calculate how long he needs to cook a turkey: $T = 35W + 20$, where T is the time in minutes and W is the weight in kilograms.

You can draw a table to find the time required for different weights of turkey.

W (kg)	4	5	6	7	8
T (min)	160	195	230	265	300

When $W = 4$, $T = 35 \times 4 + 20 = 160$
When $W = 5$, $T = 35 \times 5 + 20 = 195$
When $W = 6$, $T = 35 \times 6 + 20 = 230$

☐ Graphs from tables

You can use tables to draw graphs.

Example

Jay organises coach trips to the theatre. The table shows the cost for different numbers of people.

Number	10	20	30
Cost (£)	90	140	190

a Use the table to draw a graph.
b Use your graph to find the cost for 17 people
c What is the fixed charge for the coach?

a

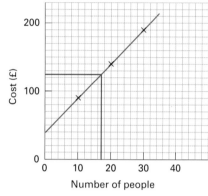

b The cost for 17 people is £125.
c The fixed charge is £40.

☐ Graphs that are curves

Not all graphs are straight lines. Some are curves.
You need to plot more points to draw a curve.
This is the table for $y = x^2 + 2$

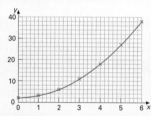

x	1	2	3	4	5	6
y	3	8	11	18	27	38

The points are plotted and joined with a curve.

Notes

The points to plot are (10, 90) (20, 140) and (30, 190).

Follow the blue line to find the cost for 17 people.

You can find the fixed charge by finding the point where the line cuts the Cost (£) axis.

Remember that x^2 means $x \times x$

When $x = 1$, $y = 1^2 + 2 = 3$
When $x = 2$, $y = 2^2 + 2 = 6$
When $x = 3$, $y = 3^2 + 2 = 11$

Join the points with a pencil to form a smooth curve.

Unit 8 pages 190–195

TEST YOURSELF

1 Lisa heats a beaker of water during an experiment.
She records the temperature each minute.
These are her results.

Time (min)	0	1	2	3	4	5
Temperature (°C)	10	31	50	63	70	75

a Copy the axes shown opposite.
b Plot the points and join them with a curve.
c Use your graph to find:
  i the temperature after 1.5 minutes
  ii how long it took to reach 55°C.

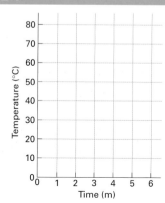

Practice questions

1 A pie costs 65 pence.
Pam buys *n* pies.
The total cost is *C* pence.
Write down a formula connecting *C* and *n*. (2)

Edexcel, 1999, Paper 1

2 Solve the following equations.

   a $4x - 5 = 7$ (2)

   b $\frac{x}{2} = -10$ (1)

   c $3(z - 2) = 27$ (3)

WJEC, 1999, Paper 2

3 A number sequence is shown.

$$1, \quad 4, \quad 9, \quad 16, \quad 25, \quad \ldots$$

   a **i** What special name is given to the numbers in this sequence? (1)

       ii What is the next number in the sequence? (1)

Patterns of black tiles and white tiles are shown.

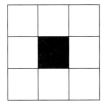 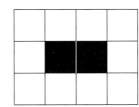 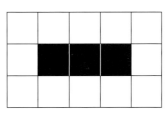

   b The number of white tiles, *w*, and the number of black tiles, *b*, are connected by the formula

$$w = 2b + 6.$$

      i In a pattern there are 18 black tiles.
        Use the formula to find the number of white tiles. (1)

      ii In another pattern there are 136 white tiles.
        Use the formula to find the number of black tiles. (2)

SEG, 1999, Paper 2

3 Shape, space and measures

- [ ] **2D shapes**
- [ ] **3D shapes**
- [ ] **Symmetry**
- [ ] **Co-ordinates**
- [ ] **Angles**
- [ ] **Transformations**
- [ ] **Measures**
- [ ] **Perimeter, area and volume**

Practice questions

2D shapes

☐ Triangles

An **equilateral triangle** has
all sides equal and all angles equal.

An **isosceles triangle** has
two equal sides and two equal angles.

The equal angles are called the *base angles*.

A **scalene triangle** has
no equal sides and no equal
angles.

A **right-angled triangle** has
an angle of *90°*.
The sides can be any lengths.

☐ Quadrilaterals

A shape with four straight sides is
called a **quadrilateral**.
A **square** has four equal sides
and four right angles.

A **rectangle** has two pairs of
equal sides and four right
angles.

A **parallelogram** has
two pairs of equal parallel sides
and two pairs of equal angles.

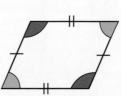

A **rhombus** has all four sides
equal, two pairs of parallel sides
and two pairs of equal angles.

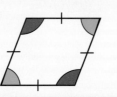

Learn the names of the different types of
triangle.

Try to learn the spellings too.

The base angles do not need to be the
angles at the bottom of the diagram. The
triangle can be turned round.

Unit 3 page 52

Learn the names of all the quadrilaterals.

Learn the facts about each of the
quadrilaterals.

A **kite** has two pairs of equal sides and one pair of equal angles.

A **trapezium** has one pair of parallel sides.
The other sides do not have to be equal.
This trapezium has two equal sides and two pairs of equal angles.

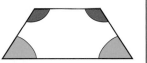

Unit 4 page 74 ➤

☐ Naming polygons

A **polygon** is a shape with straight sides.
A polygon with **3** sides is called a **triangle**.
A polygon with **4** sides is called a **quadrilateral**.
A polygon with **5** sides is called a **pentagon**.
A polygon with **6** sides is called a **hexagon**.
A polygon with **7** sides is called a **heptagon**.
A polygon with **8** sides is called an **octagon**.
A polygon with **10** sides is called a **decagon**.
A polygon with **12** sides is called a **dodecagon**.

A **regular polygon** has all its sides equal and all its angles equal.
This is a regular hexagon.

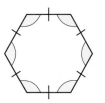

Notes

Learn all the names of these well-known polygons.

You will probably only need to remember the names for polygons with 3, 4, 5, 6 and 8 sides. You may see the other names on your exam paper.

Unit 3 page 54 ➤

TEST YOURSELF

1 Copy these shapes.

Write the name of each shape underneath.

a

b

c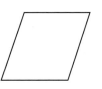

d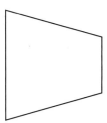

2 Copy these sentences and complete them.

  a A regular triangle is an _____ triangle.
  b A regular quadrilateral is a _____ .

3 Draw each of these shapes:

  a a kite
  b a scalene triangle
  c a regular pentagon
  d a regular octagon
  e a right-angled isosceles triangle.

☐ Congruence

> Two shapes are **congruent** if they are identical.
> They must be exactly the same size and shape.

Example

These two squares are
congruent.
They are exactly the same
size and shape.

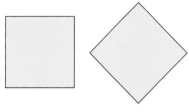

This square is not
congruent to the other two.
It is not the same size.

☐ Tessellation

> A tessellation is a pattern made by repeating the
> same shape over and over again.
>
> There are no gaps in a tessellation.
>
>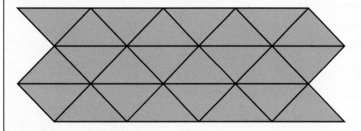
>
> This is a tessellation made from triangles.

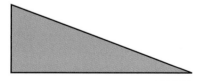

Notes

Remember that congruent is another word
for identical.

Unit 4 pages 72–75

All quadrilaterals tessellate. This is because
all triangles tessellate. Turn one over and
make a quadrilateral with the two triangles,
as in this picture.

Unit 4 pages 76–77

TEST YOURSELF

1 Write down the letters of all the congruent
pairs of shapes

A   B   C   D

E   F   G   H

I    J

2 Draw a tessellation of each of these
shapes.

a

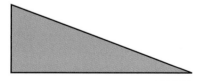

b

48

3D shapes

☐ Solids

This is a cuboid.

A cuboid has 6 faces,
12 edges and 8 vertices.

A prism is a solid that has
the same shape all the way
through.
This shape is called the
cross-section of the prism.
The cross-section must be
a polygon.

A plane is a flat surface.

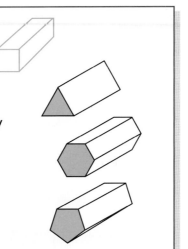

Notes

A face is one of the surfaces of the solid.
An edge is where two faces meet.
A vertex is where two edges meet.
The plural of vertex is vertices.

A polygon is a shape that has straight lines
for all its edges.

Examples

This is a prism.
The *cross-section* is a triangle.
So this solid is a triangular prism.
This solid has 5 faces, 9 edges and
6 vertices.
All the faces are planes.

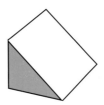

Learn the names of the different types of
solid shapes.

The shape of the cross-section gives you the
full name of the prism.

This is a pyramid.
It has a square base.
It is a square-based pyramid.
It has 5 faces, 8 edges and 5 vertices.
All the faces are planes.

The shape of the base gives you the full
name of the pyramid.

This is a cone.
It has 2 faces, 1 edge and 1 vertex.
It has one **plane face**
and one *curved face*.

The one edge of a cone is a circle.

This is a cylinder.
It is not a prism because the
cross-section is a circle
and not a polygon.

A cylinder has 2 **plane faces** and
one *curved face*.

A cylinder has two circular edges.
It has no vertices.

This is a sphere.
It has one curved face.

A sphere has no edges and no vertices.

Unit 1 pages 2–4

☐ Nets

When a solid is opened out and laid flat, the shape that you get is called a **net** of the solid.

    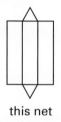

This solid   gives   this net

☐ Drawing

You can draw solid shapes like you have already seen on the last page.

You can also use isometric paper to draw cuboids.

Use these 3 directions to draw the edges of the shape.

The lengths of the edges of a cuboid are the same when drawn on isometric paper.

This is a cuboid that is 4 cm by 3 cm by 2 cm.

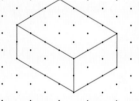

Notes

You don't put flaps on a net unless you're going to make the solid.

Unit 1 page 7 ➡

Make sure that the isometric paper is the right way up.

This is right.   This is wrong.

Unit 2 pages 24–27 ➡

TEST YOURSELF

1 Write down the number of:

a faces

b edges

c vertices

of this square based pyramid.

2 Write down the name of each of these solids.

a   **b**

3 Draw a net of each of these solids:

a cube

b square based pyramid

c cylinder.

4 Draw this cuboid on isometric paper.

2 cm
5 cm
4 cm

50

Symmetry

☐ Lines of symmetry

A line of symmetry divides a shape into two identical halves.

Each part is a reflection of the other. If you fold a shape along a line of symmetry the two parts will fit exactly on top of each other.

This shape has 2 lines of symmetry.

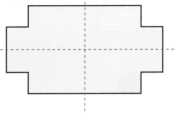

The lines of symmetry are shown by the red dashed lines.

Examples

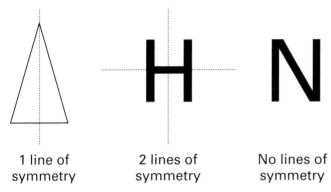

| 1 line of symmetry | 2 lines of symmetry | No lines of symmetry |

☐ Drawing reflections

Reflect a point in a mirror line by drawing a line at right angles to the mirror from the point.

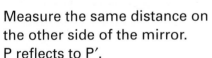

Measure the same distance on the other side of the mirror. P reflects to P′.

Draw reflections of shapes by working with each vertex in turn. Then join the new points together to give the reflected shape.

Example

Triangle A′B′C′ is the reflection of triangle ABC in the mirror line.

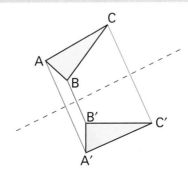

Notes

A line of symmetry is sometimes called a mirror line.

A line of symmetry is always drawn as a dashed line.

Unit 5 pages 98–101

You can use tracing paper to do reflections.

- Trace the shape and the mirror line using a pencil.
- Turn the tracing paper over.
- Put the traced mirror line on top of the actual mirror line.
- Draw over the back of the shape on the tracing paper and when you take the tracing paper away you will have the reflection drawn.

You are allowed to ask for tracing paper in your exam.

☐ Rotational symmetry

A shape has rotational symmetry if it looks the same as you rotate it around its centre.

The order of rotational symmetry is the number of times that the shape looks the same as it makes one complete turn.

If a shape doesn't look the same at least twice then it does not have rotational symmetry but you can say it has order 1 rotational symmetry.

Examples

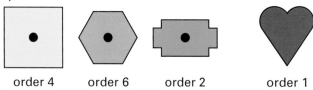

| order 4 | order 6 | order 2 | order 1 |

Regular polygons have rotational symmetry and line symmetry.

The number of sides tells you the number of lines of symmetry and the order of rotational symmetry.

 Regular polygons page 47

☐ Symmetry in 3D

Symmetry still works for 3D shapes. Instead of a line of symmetry you now have a plane of symmetry.

Here are the planes of symmetry for a cuboid.

 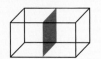 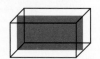

Notes

The order of rotational symmetry is just a mathematical way of saying the number of times the picture looks the same as you rotate it.

You can use tracing paper to find the order of rotational symmetry.

● Trace the shape and the centre of rotation.
● Hold the centre still with a pencil.
● Rotate the tracing paper and count how many times the shape looks the same as you make one complete turn.

You are allowed to ask for tracing paper in your exam.

A regular hexagon has 6 lines of symmetry and rotational symmetry of order 6.

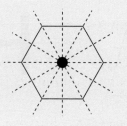

Unit 6 page 142

A plane is a flat surface. So think of a mirror when looking at a plane of symmetry.

Unit 6 page 144

TEST YOURSELF

1 Copy these shapes. For each shape:
   a draw all the lines of symmetry
   b write down the order of rotational symmetry.

A   B   C

D   E   F

2 Copy this diagram. Draw the reflection of triangle ABC in the dashed mirror line.

3 Copy these shapes. Draw all the planes of symmetry. Use a separate diagram for each.

A   B

Equilateral triangular prism

Square based pyramid

Co-ordinates

☐ First quadrant

Co-ordinates are used to describe the position of something.

The starting point is called the origin, O.

Then you say how far across to the right and how far up to go.

P is **2** squares across from O and *3* squares up.
The co-ordinates of P are (**2**, *3*).
Q is **0** squares across from O and *2* squares up.
The co-ordinates of Q are (**0**, *2*).
R is **4** squares across from O and *0* squares up.
The co-ordinates of R are (**4**, *0*).

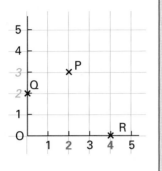

Notes

Always give the across co-ordinate first.
The across co-ordinate
is called the x co-ordinate.
The up co-ordinate
is called the y co-ordinate.

Put co-ordinates in brackets.
Put a comma in between.

Unit 7 pages 152–153

☐ All 4 quadrants

You can move left and down as well as right and up in co-ordinates.

You use negative numbers.

A is **4** squares *left* of O and *2* squares *down*.
The co-ordinates of A are
(**−4**, *−2*).
B is **3** squares *left* of O and *4* squares up.
The co-ordinates of B are
(**−3**, *4*).
C is **2** squares *right* of O and *3* squares *down*.
The co-ordinates of C are (**2**, *−3*).

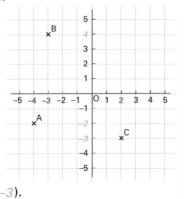

Unit 10 page 225

TEST YOURSELF

1 Write down the co-ordinates of the points marked.

2 Copy the axes in question **1** onto squared paper.

Plot these points.

P(1, 4)   Q(1, 0)   R(0, 3)   S(−1, −2)

T(−3, −4)   U(−1, 5)   V(4, −5)   W(3, −1)

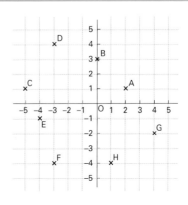

Angles

☐ Drawing and measuring

Angles are measured in degrees.
There are 360° in a full turn.

You can use a protractor to measure angles.
It has two scales.

It has a clockwise scale
on the outside and
an anticlockwise
scale on the inside.

It also has a cross
and a zero line.

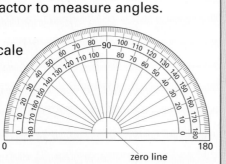

zero line

Always make sure that one side of the angle is on
the zero line of the protractor. Read the angle on
the scale that starts at zero.

Use the blue scale
The angle JKL is 45°.

Use the red scale.
The angle PQR is 130°.

To draw an angle of 60° at P.

(1) Draw a horizontal line.
(2) Put a small × at P.
(3) Put the cross of the
    protractor on the ×.
    The zero line of the
    protractor must lie on
    the horizontal line.
(4) Find 60° on the clockwise scale.
(5) Make a mark at this point.
(6) Join the × to this mark with
    a straight line.
(7) Label the angle 60°.

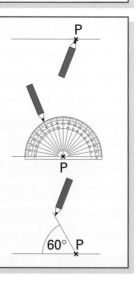

Notes

Remember that this direction is clockwise

. . . this is the way that the hands on a clock
move. . .

and this direction is anticlockwise

. . . this is the opposite way.

Always make sure that you read from the
scale that starts at zero.

Also think about the size of the angle.
An acute angle must be less than 90°.

An obtuse angle must be between 90° and
180°.

A reflex angle must be bigger than 180°.

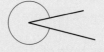

Unit 8 pages 177–180

TEST YOURSELF

1 Use the diagram to find the size of these
angles.

a AP̂B	**c** AP̂D	**e** ZP̂B	**g** ZP̂D
b AP̂C	**d** AP̂E	**f** ZP̂C	**h** ZP̂E

2 Draw these angles:

a 45°	**c** 120°	**e** 105°	**g** 270°
b 78°	**d** 143°	**f** 171°	**h** 230°

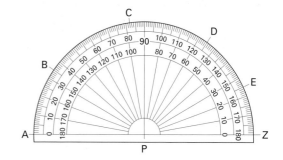

☐ Angles on a straight line

Angles on a straight line add up to 180°.

$a = 180° - 65°$
$\quad = 115°$

65° a

☐ Angles round a point

Angles round a point add up to 360°.

$b = 360° - 125°$
$\quad = 235°$

125°
b

☐ Angles in a triangle

Angles in a triangle add up to 180°.

$52° + 37° = 89°$
$c = 180° - 89°$
$\quad = 91°$

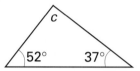

c

52°   37°

☐ Angles in a quadrilateral

Angles in a quadrilateral add up to 360°.

$36° + 56° + 122° = 214°$
$d = 360° - 214°$
$\quad = 146°$

d   122°

36°   56°

☐ Opposite angles

Angles that are opposite each other in a cross are equal.
g is opposite the 57°
so $g = 57°$.
$e = 180° - 57° = 123°$.
$f = e = 123°$.

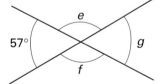

e

57°   g

f

Notes

Learn these important results and how to work out angles like this.

You won't be able to measure angles in questions that want you to use these results.

Add up the angles you know.
Take the total away from 180°.

Add up the angles you know.
Take the total away from 360°.

The angle e is on a straight line with the 57° angle.
e and f are opposite angles.

Unit 18 pages 423–426

TEST YOURSELF

1 Calculate the angles marked with letters.

a

81° a

b

160°
b

123°

c

93°

c   64°

d

d
100°

80°   95°

e

f
72°   e
g

f

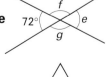

70°

h   h

g

81°

i

h

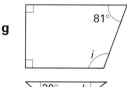

30°   k
j

130°

☐ Angles in parallel lines

You can use opposite angles and angles on a
straight line to work out the angles in parallel lines.

Angles *a* and *b* are equal
because they are opposite.

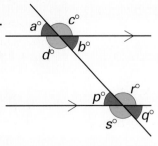

The sloping line cuts the
bottom line at the same
angle as the top line.

So *p* and *q* are the same
as *a* and *b*.

You can find angle *c* by working out 180° − *a*
because the angles *a* and *c* are on a straight line.

When you know angle *c* you know all the rest of
the angles too. Angles *d*, *r* and *s* are all equal to *c*.

☐ Angles in polygons

An interior angle is an angle
inside a shape where two
sides meet.

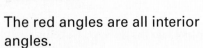

The red angles are all interior
angles.

An exterior angle is an angle
outside a shape where two
sides meet.

But it is not the whole angle
outside.

You need to make one side longer and look at the
angle between this new line and the next side.

The blue angles are all exterior angles.

The exterior angles of a polygon add up to 360°.

If a polygon is regular all of the
exterior angles are the same.

For this regular pentagon

$$\text{exterior angle} = \frac{360}{5} = 72°$$

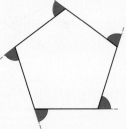

Notes

The proper name for angles that are the
same because they are in the same place on
the cross at the top and at the bottom is
corresponding angles.

Angles *a* and *p* are corresponding angles.
Angles *c* and *r* are also corresponding
angles. You don't need to know the name of
these angles but you do need to know that
they are equal.

A polygon is any shape with straight sides.

A corner of a polygon is called a vertex.

At a corner of any polygon the interior angle and the exterior angle add up to 180° because they are on a straight line.

So interior angle = 180° − exterior angle.

For this regular hexagon:

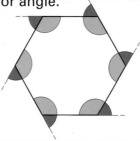

$$\text{exterior angle} = \frac{360}{6} = 60°$$

$$\text{interior angle} = 180° - 60°$$
$$= 120°$$

 See also **Naming polygons** page 47

☐ Points of the compass

There are 8 points of the compass. There is 45° between each pair of directions.

☐ Bearings

A bearing is an angle.
It tells you the direction of one place from another.

To give a bearing you must face North and turn clockwise.

A bearing has 3 figures.

The bearing of Bedford from Abingdon is 047°.

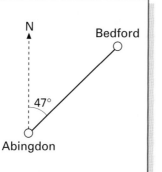

Notes

Always work with the exterior angle first. Then take it away from 180° to find the interior angle.

Unit 18 pages 427–430

When a question says the bearing of A from B it means that you are at B. You face North and turn clockwise until you are facing A. The angle you turn through is the bearing.

Unit 8 pages 180–182

TEST YOURSELF

1 Calculate the angles marked with letters.

a

b

c

d

e

f

2 How many degrees are there between:

a N and E   **d** NW and S
b S and SE   **e** NW and E
c E and SW   **f** SE and NE?

3 Find the bearing of A from B.

a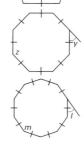

b

c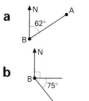

d

Transformations

☐ Object and image

> The shape that you start with is called the object.
>
> The shape that you get after a transformation has been done is called the image.

☐ Reflection

> A reflection is what you see when you look in a mirror.
>
> When you reflect an object every point moves the same distance on the other side of the mirror. Every point moves across at right angles to the mirror.

Example

Triangle A'B'C' is the reflection of triangle ABC in the *y* axis.

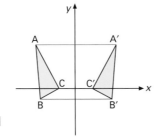

 Symmetry page 51

☐ Rotation

> A rotation turns a shape around a fixed point.
>
> The fixed point is called the centre of the rotation.
>
> To rotate a shape about a point:
>
> (1) you need to know the angle and the direction of turn
> (2) trace the shape and the centre
> (3) put a cross at the centre (this is helpful to see rotations of 90°, 180° and 270° when the cross will look the same as when it started)
> (4) put your pencil on the centre of the rotation and rotate the tracing paper
> (5) draw the shape in its new position.

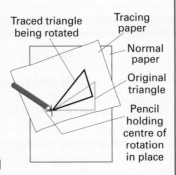

Traced triangle being rotated

Tracing paper

Normal paper

Original triangle

Pencil holding centre of rotation in place

Notes

When you describe any transformation you need to look at the object first. You need to say what has happened to it to make it become the image.

You can use tracing paper to do reflections.

- Trace the shape and the mirror line using a pencil.
- Turn the tracing paper over.
- Put the traced mirror line on top of the actual mirror line.
- Draw over the back of the shape on the tracing paper and when you take the tracing paper away you will have the reflection drawn.

You are allowed to ask for tracing paper in your exam.

When you describe a reflection you must say where the mirror line is.

You can draw the line on a diagram and say that the line you have drawn is the mirror line or you can give the equation of the mirror line. Watch out for these two diagonal mirrors.

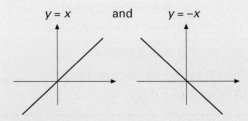

When you describe a rotation you must give these **three** things:

- the centre – give this using co-ordinates
- the angle that you rotate the shape and
- the direction that you turn – clockwise or anticlockwise.

Again make sure that you ask for tracing paper if you want to use it in your exam.

Unit 10 pages 224–227

☐ Translation

A translation is a movement in a straight line.
The image must look exactly the same as the
object.

Notes

When you describe a translation you need to
say how far to the right or left and how far
up or down the object has moved to get to
the image.

Example

Triangle A'B'C' is a
translation of
triangle ABC.

ABC has been moved
3 places to the right and
2 places up.

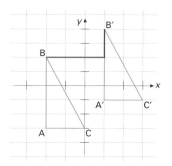

☐ Enlargements

An enlargement is the only
transformation that changes
the size of the object.

Look at the corner of the small
triangle marked ●

● is 1 square from C.

After an enlargement, scale
factor 3 centre C, ● on the image
is 3 squares from C.

The other corners work the same way.

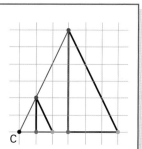

When you describe an enlargement you must
give these **two** things:

● the centre of the enlargement – give this
using co-ordinates
● the scale factor of the enlargement –
this is how many times bigger the image
is than the object.

Unit 15 pages 342–346 ⟩

TEST YOURSELF

1 Copy this diagram onto squared paper.
Draw the image of triangle *A* after:

  a reflection in the *y* axis
  b reflection in *y = x*
  c rotation about O through 90° clockwise
  d translation 3 to the right and 1 down
  e translation 6 to the left and 3 down
  f reflection in *y = −x*
  g rotation through 180° about O.

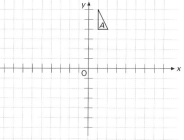

2 Write down the letter of the image of
shape *P* after

  a reflection in the *x* axis
  b rotation about O through 180°
  c translation 4 to the left and 5 up
  d rotation about O through 90° anticlockwise
  e reflection in *x = 5*
  f enlargement centre O factor 2.

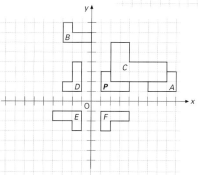

Measures

☐ Reading scales

Look at this scale for distance on a map.

0   20   km

There are 5 gaps from 0 to 20 so each gap is
20 ÷ 5 = 4 km.

Two gaps along from zero is 2 × 4 = 8.
(So the pointer is at 8.)

Example

What is the mass shown by the
pointer?
The difference between 7 and 8 is 1.
There are 4 small gaps from 7 to 8
so each gap is 1 ÷ 4 = 0.25 kg.
The pointer is 3 gaps along.
The mass is 7 + (3 × 0.25) = 7.75 kg.

7 kg   8 kg

☐ Scale drawing

This is a scale drawing of Jessica's lounge.

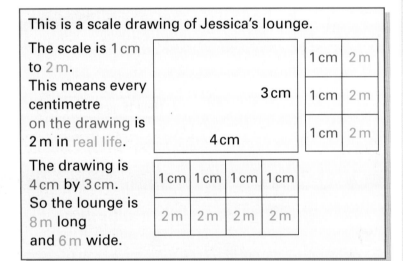

The scale is 1 cm
to 2 m.
This means every
centimetre
on the drawing is
2 m in real life.

1 cm	2 m
1 cm	2 m
1 cm	2 m

3 cm

4 cm

The drawing is
4 cm by 3 cm.
So the lounge is
8 m long
and 6 m wide.

1 cm	1 cm	1 cm	1 cm
2 m	2 m	2 m	2 m

Example

Here is a technical drawing of a metal plate.
The drawing uses a scale of 1 : 50.
Find the length of:
a AB **b** HI in real life.

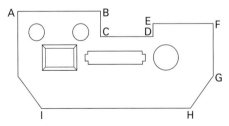

The scale means 1 cm on the drawing is 50 cm in real life.
AB = 2.3 × 50 = 115 cm = 1 m 15 cm
HI = 4.1 × 50 = 205 cm = 2 m 5 cm

Notes

Sometimes the gaps on the scale are called divisions.

Each gap is $\frac{1}{4}$ of a unit.

You take the 7 kg at the beginning of the scale and add on 3 gaps of 0.25 kg.

Drawings like this are often called plans.

Scales like 1 : 50 are sometimes referred to as map ratios. This is just the same as a scale of 1 cm to 50 cm.

Ordnance survey maps with pink covers have map ratios of 1 : 50 000.
This means 1 cm on the map is 50 000 cm in real life.
50 000 cm is 50 000 ÷ 100 = 500 m.
So every cm on a map like this is 500 m in real life.

☐ Constructing triangles

How you draw a triangle depends on what information you are given.

Notes

Examples

a Make an accurate drawing of the triangle shown. Use a scale of 1 cm to 1 m.

First draw the base 6 cm long.

Next use a protractor to measure the angles.

Finally make the sides longer until they cross.

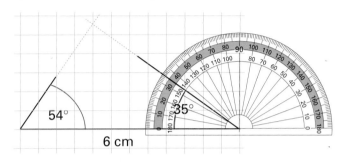

Questions on drawing triangles always give you at least one side. This is because you cannot draw **one** triangle if you are just given the angles.

These two triangles have the same angles but they are different sizes.

b Draw a triangle with sides 5 cm, 4 cm and 2 cm.

Start with the base.

Draw an arc radius 4 cm from A.

Draw an arc radius 2 cm from B to cross the first one.

Join A and B to where the arcs cross.

It is best to use the longest side as a base.

TEST YOURSELF

1 Write down the values shown by the pointers

a

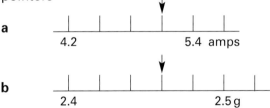

b

2 What are the lengths of the sides of this garden in real life? The scale is 1 cm to 100 m.

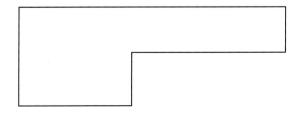

3 This is a rough plan of a new park. *AB* = 900 m.

a Make a scale drawing of the park. Use a scale of 1 cm to 200 m.
b What is the perimeter of the park?

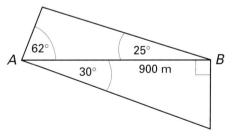

4 Draw a triangle with sides 6 cm, 5 cm and 3 cm.
Measure the angles in the triangle.

5 Draw a triangle with sides 4 cm, 3 cm and 2 cm.

☐ Changing between metric units

The conversions you need to know are
1 cm = 10 mm   1 g = 1000 mg   1 l = 100 cl
1 m = 100 cm   1 kg = 1000 g   1 l = 1000 ml
1 km = 1000 m   1 t = 1000 kg

Examples

1 Change: **a** 320 cm to m   **b** 7.4 km to m.
a Each metre is 100 cm
    320 cm = 320 ÷ 100 = 3.2 m
b Each kilometre is 1000 m
    7.4 km = 7.4 × 1000 = 7400 m
2 Change: **a** 4650 g to kg   **b** 2.4 t to kg.
a Each kilogram is 1000 g
    4650 g = 4650 ÷ 1000 = 4.65 kg
b Each tonne is 1000 kg
    2.4 t = 2.4 × 1000 = 2400 kg
3 Change: **a** 2.7 l to ml   **b** 75 cl to l.
a Each litre is 1000 ml
    2.7 l = 2.7 × 1000 = 2700 ml
b Each litre is 100 cl
    75 cl = 75 ÷ 100 = 0.75 l

☐ Changing between metric and imperial units

You can use conversion numbers for this.

From imperial, × by the conversion number to get metric.

From metric, ÷ by the conversion number to get imperial.

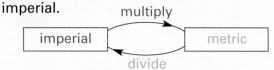

multiply / imperial / metric / divide

For **lengths** use these conversion numbers.

1 in is about 2.5 cm.   1 ft is about 30 cm.
1 yd is about 90 cm.   1 mile is about 1.6 km.

For **masses** use these conversion numbers.

1 oz is about 30 g.   1 lb is about 450 g.
1 st is about 6.5 kg.

For **capacities** use these conversion numbers.

1 pt is about 600 ml.   1 gal is about 4.5 l.

Notes

The units in red are lengths.
The units in blue are masses.
The units in green are capacities.

Remember that an adult is a bit less than 2 m tall. A standard size tin of baked beans is about ½ kg whereas a baked bean is about a gram. A small car is about a tonne. A tall carton of milk is a litre and a centimetre cube of milk is a millilitre.

Always state the conversion before you do any multiplying or dividing. Ask yourself if the conversion looks sensible from your everyday knowledge of units.

Always ask yourself if there will be more or less when you have changed units.

For example, if you change 5 cm to mm there will obviously be more in mm. This means you will need to multiply.

On the other hand if you change 50 mm to cm, you will obviously have less in cm. This means you will need to divide.

Common imperial units are:

length	1 foot (ft) = 12 inches (in)
	1 yard (yd) = 3 feet
	1 mile = 1760 yards
mass	1 pound (lb) = 16 ounces (oz)
	1 stone (st) = 14 pounds
capacity	1 gallon (gal) = 8 pints (pt)

TEST YOURSELF

1 Change each of these to the units shown:

   a 4 m to cm   **b** 6.2 km to m
   c 85 mm to cm   **d** 7800 m to km
   e 4800 mg to g   **f** 2.9 g to mg
   g 94 000 kg to t   **h** 5.85 kg to g
   i 45 cl to l   **j** 2300 ml to l
   k 2.5 l to cl   **l** 0.45 l to ml

2 Convert each of these into the units shown:

   a 4 in into cm   **b** 150 cm into ft
   c 16 km into miles   **d** 60 cm into in
   e 4 oz into g   **f** 900 g into lb
   g 10 st into kg   **h** 240 g into oz
   i 5 pt into ml   **j** 6 gal into l
   k 2400 ml into pt   **l** 90 l into gal

☐ Time

To work out time in days or weeks draw a calendar.

Example

June has to go to hospital on Tuesday 17th May. Her next appointment is 16 days later. What day and date is this?

Draw a calendar.
Put in Tues 17th.
Count on 16 days.
May has 31 days.

Mon	Tue	Wed	Thur	Fri	Sat	Sun
	17	18^1	19^2	20^3	21^4	22^5
23^6	24^7	25^8	26^9	27^{10}	28^{11}	29^{12}
30^{13}	31^{14}	1^{15}	2^{16}	3	4	5

So June's next appointment is Thursday 2nd June.

To work out a gap between times, you can use a time line.

Example

Jim is a lorry driver. He sets off from Dover at 09.50
He reaches Thame 2 h 50 min later. What time is this?

10 min 10,00   1 hour   11,00   1 hour   12,00   40 min   13,00

09.50   12.40

From 09.50 to 10.00 is 10 min.

2 h 50 min − 10 min = 2 h 40 min.

From 10.00 to 12.00 is 2 h.

2 h 40 min − 2 h = 40 min.

Jim arrives in Thame at 12.40.

☐ Average speed

Average speed = $\dfrac{\text{Distance}}{\text{Time}}$

Examples

1 A boat leaves Portsmouth for Cherbourg. It takes 5 hours to travel 100 km. What is its average speed?

The distance is 100 km. The time is 5 hours.

Average speed = $\dfrac{100}{5}$ The distance is in km
                                          the time is in hours

= 20 km/h   so the units are km/h

2 A man runs 30 m in 4 s. What is his average speed?

Average speed = $\dfrac{30}{4}$ The distance is in m
                                          the time is in seconds

= 7.5 m/s   so the units are m/s

Notes

You need to know how many days are in each month. There is a poem which helps.

It begins: '30 days has September, April, June and November. . .'

You can then remember that all the rest have 31, except February which has 28.

However, every 4 years February has 29. This is called a leap year. The year 2000 was a leap year.

You could do the date example in another way.

Add 16 onto the 17

16 + 17 = 33, but there are only 31 days in May. 33 − 31 = 2. This gives 2nd June.

Another way to do this example is to add the times together. If you do this, you must remember that there are only 60 minutes in an hour.

You would add the hours first:

9 + 2 = 11

Then add the minutes:

50 + 50 = 100

There are 60 minutes in an hour so,

100 min = 1 h 40 min

11.00 + 1 h 40 min = 12.40

Unit 15 page 349

☐ Travel graphs

The graph below shows Freda's train journey to London.

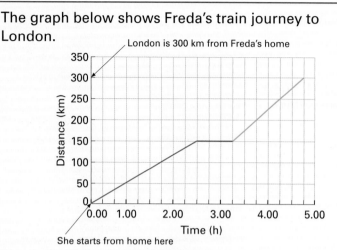

London is 300 km from Freda's home

She starts from home here

The first part of the journey is the red line.
The graph slopes upwards.
Freda is on a slow train, going away from her house.
She travels 150 km in 2 h 30 min.

The second part of the journey is the blue line.
The graph is horizontal.
This means that Freda is not moving.
Freda gets off the first train and waits at a station.

The last part of the journey is the green line.
The speed here is zero.
The graph slopes upwards.
She is going faster in this part.
The line is steeper than in the first part.
Freda is on a fast train moving away from home.
She travels the last 150 km in 1½ hours.

Notes

The graph below shows a journey where someone sets out from home, stops for a while, then returns home.

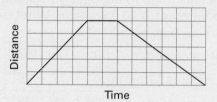

A line which *slopes down* towards the horizontal axis means that someone is returning towards where they started.

You can work out the average speed of the first part of Freda's journey.

$$\text{Average speed} = \frac{150}{2\frac{1}{2}} = 60\,\text{km/h}$$

In this section, no distance is covered, but $\frac{3}{4}$ of an hour goes by.

You can work out the average speed of the last part.

$$\text{Average speed} = \frac{150}{1\frac{1}{2}} = 100\,\text{km/h}$$

The overall average speed is $\frac{300}{4\frac{3}{4}}$

$$= 63.2\,\text{km/h}$$

TEST YOURSELF

1   Charlie has to go to the optician on Friday 12th November. His next appointment is 27 days later. What day and date is this?

2   Maureen works for an airline. She catches a plane from Toronto at 07.30. She arrives in Vancouver 3 h 47 min later. What time is this?

3   Bernard catches a train from London to York.
    The train takes 5 hours to travel 300 km.
    What is the average speed of the train?

4   A rocket travels 480 miles in 40 seconds. What is its average speed in miles per second?

5   The graph shows Paul's journey from Wiltshire to Kent. First he catches a fast train, then a tube, then a slow train.

    a   How long does he spend on the tube?
    b   Work out the average speed of each train journey.

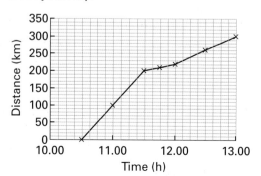

Perimeter, area and volume

☐ Perimeter

> The perimeter is the total distance around the outside of a shape.

Example

Find the perimeter of these shapes

a
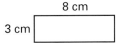
8 cm
3 cm

b
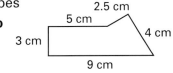
2.5 cm
5 cm
3 cm
4 cm
9 cm

This shape is a rectangle. Mark on the lengths of the other 2 sides.
Mark the start with an arrow.

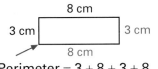
8 cm
3 cm   3 cm
8 cm

Mark the start with an arrow. Now add up all the sides.

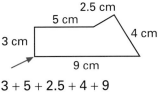
2.5 cm
5 cm
3 cm
4 cm
9 cm

Perimeter = 3 + 8 + 3 + 8
= 6 + 16 = 22 cm

3 + 5 + 2.5 + 4 + 9
= 23.5 cm

☐ Area by counting

> The area of a shape is the space it covers.
> If a shape is split into squares you can count its area.
> There are **10** whole squares and **4** half squares here.
>
> So the area is $10 + 4 \times \frac{1}{2}$
> $= 10 + 2$
> $= 12\ \text{cm}^2$

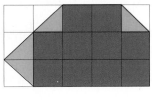

☐ Area of rectangles and triangles

> The area of a rectangle is: length × width
>
> The area of a triangle is: (base × height) ÷ 2

Example

Find the area of each of these shapes.

a
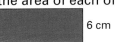
6 cm
9 cm

b

4 m
8 m

a Area = length × width
Area = 9 × 6
Area = 54 cm²

b Area = (base × height) ÷ 2
Area = (8 × 4) ÷ 2
Area = 32 ÷ 2 = 16 cm²

Notes

It is a good idea to mark where you start from with an arrow. The arrow reminds you not to miss a side out. It also helps to stop you counting a side twice.

A common mistake when finding the perimeter of a rectangle is to forget to put in the lengths of any missing sides.

You could find the perimeter of the rectangle by doing   2 × 3 + 2 × 8
= 6 + 16
= 22 cm

1 cm
1 cm
The area of this shape is 1 cm².

Be careful to tick the areas off in a shape like this to make sure you don't miss any.

A square is a special rectangle where the length equals the width.
So the area of a square is length × length.

Triangles can be shown in different positions. With these, you need to look for a height that is at right angles to the base. In the triangles below, the base is marked **b** and the height is marked **h**.

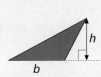
h
b

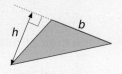
h
b

TEST YOURSELF

1 Find the perimeter of these shapes in metres.

a

2.4 m
50 cm
0.8 m
1.2 m
40 cm
1 m

b

25 cm

2 Find the area of each of these shapes in m².

a
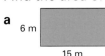
6 m
15 m

b
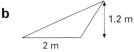
1.2 m
2 m

☐ Circumference of a circle

> The circumference is the distance round the edge of a circle.
> It is '3 and a little bit' times the diameter.
> This number is called π. It is very near to 3.14.
> The formula is **Circumference = π × diameter**

Example

Find the circumference of a circle with a radius of 10 cm.

The diameter is 2 × the radius,
so the diameter is 2 × 10 = 20 cm.
Circumference = π × diameter
So circumference = π × 20 = 62.831...
= 62.8 cm (to 1 decimal place)

radius 10 cm

☐ Area of a circle

> The area is the space inside a circle.
>
> If you square the radius, you get a square like this:
>
>
>
> You can see that 4 of these squares are too big for the area of a circle.
>
> But π times the square of the radius is just right!
>
> So the formula is **Area = π × radius × radius**

Example

Find the area of a circle with a diameter of 10 cm.
The diameter is 2 × the radius,
so the radius is 10 ÷ 2 = 5 cm.

Area   = π × radius × radius
So area = π × 5 × 5 = 78.539... = 78.5 cm² (1 d.p.)

☐ Area of combined shapes

> If shapes are combined, you work out each area separately.

Example

Find the area of this shape:

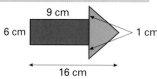

Split the shape into a rectangle and a triangle.
Work out any missing lengths that you need.

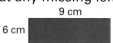

Area of rectangle   = 6 × 9   = 54 cm²
Area of a triangle = (7 × 8) ÷ 2 = <u>28 cm²</u>
Total area   = 82 cm²

66

Notes

The circumference is *very roughly* 3 times the diameter. You can use this to check that your answer is about right.

You may remember that π is a never ending number. Its decimal places go on forever! You can get a very good value from your calculator. Press your $\boxed{\pi}$ button to get π = 3.141592654. . .

π × 20 is best done on your calculator:

The area is *very roughly* 3 times the radius squared. You can use this to check that your answer is about right.

You may be asked to find the area of a semicircle.
The best thing to do is find the area of the whole circle and divide it by 2.

This ⌓ is half of this! ◯

Here the radius squared is 5 × 5 = 25
So a rough estimate would be
3 × 25 = 75 cm²

You key in
to get the exact answer.

The base of the triangle = 6 + 1 + 1 = 8 cm
The height of the triangle = 16 − 9 = 7 cm

☐ Volume and capacity

Volume is the amount of space a solid takes up.
Capacity is the amount of space in a hollow object.

This cube has a volume of 1 cm³.
All its sides are 1 cm long.

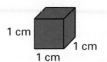

1 cm
1 cm
1 cm

Look at this shape. If you count
the cubes there are 12.
So the volume is 12 cm³.

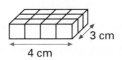

3 cm
4 cm

But you can also do length × width = 4 × 3 = 12 cm³.

This shape is similar, but there
are 2 layers.
The volume is the number in a
layer × height.
The volume is 4 × 3 × 2 = 24 cm³.

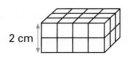

2 cm

So **Volume of a cuboid** = length × width × height

Notes

A mountain has volume.
A fuel tank has capacity.
A cube with all its sides 1 m long has a
volume of 1 m³.

If a cube like this is
hollow and filled
with water, it has a
capacity of 1 ml.

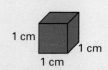

1 cm
1 cm
1 cm

A cube is a special sort of cuboid.
All its lengths are the same.
You can write:
   Volume
   of a cube = length × length × length

or   Volume of a cube = (length)³

Here Volume = 5³ = 125 m³

Examples

1 Find the volume of a cube
   with a side length of 5 m.

5 m
5 m
5 m

   The length is 5 m, the width is 5 m and the height is 5 m
   So the volume is 5 × 5 × 5 = 125 m³.

2 Find the capacity of this perfume bottle
   in ml.
   The part that holds the liquid is a cuboid.

   Volume of the bottle = 6.2 × 3.4 × 8.7
                        = 183.396 cm³
   Every cm³ = 1 ml so capacity = 183.4 ml to 1 d.p.

8.7 cm
6.2 cm   3.4 cm

T E S T   Y O U R S E L F

1 Find the circumference of each of these
   circles.
   Round your answers to 1 d.p. Use your
   π button.

   a   **b**   **c**
   25 cm   4.5 m   2.7 cm

2 Find the area of each of these circles.
   Round your answers to 2 d.p. Use your
   π button.

   a   **b**   **c**
   4 cm   17.3 m   4.8 m

3 Find the area of this garden in m².

16 m
25 m

4 Find the volume of these shapes in m³.
   Round your answers to 2 d.p.

   a 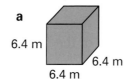   **b**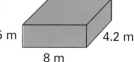

6.4 m   1.5 m   4.2 m
        6.4 m   8 m
6.4 m

Practice questions

1

Diagram **NOT** accurately drawn

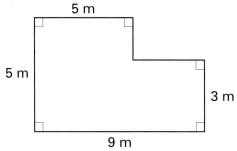

This diagram shows the floor plan of a room.

Work out the area of the floor.
Give the units with your answer.   (4)

Edexcel, 1999, Paper 2

2

Diagram **NOT** accurately drawn

AB is parallel to *DC*.

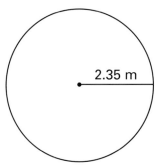

a Work out the size of angle *x*.
Give a reason for your answer.   (2)

b Work out the size of angle *y*.
Give a reason for your answer.   (2)

NEAB, 1999, Paper 2

3

A circular table has a radius of 2.35 m. The top of the table is painted with varnish.
One litre of varnish covers 4 m².

a How many litre tins of varnish must be bought to paint the top of the table?   (4)

b What is the circumference of the top of the table?   (2)

WJEC, 1999, Paper 1

4 Handling data

☐ **Averages and range**

☐ **Probability**

☐ **Diagrams**

Averages and range

☐ Range

> You can obtain the **range** of a set of data by subtracting the smallest value from the largest value.
>
> Your answer must be given as a single value and not left as a subtraction sum.
>
> The range tells you how wide the gap is between the largest and the smallest values.

You must remember that the range is always given as a single value.

Example

Jenny recorded how late her train was each day last week. This is what she wrote down.

| Mon 13 min | Tues 4 min | Wed 8 min |
| Thur 17 min | Fri 8 min | |

The range of these times is 17 − 4 = 13 min.

Unit 13 pages 301–305

☐ Mean

> To work out the **mean** of a set of data:
>
> **1** add together all the data values
>
> **2** divide the total by the number of data values.

Example

To find the mean number of minutes Jenny's train was late:

1 add the times together

2 divide by five.

The total is 13 + 4 + 8 + 17 + 8 = 50
The mean is 50 ÷ 5 = 10 min.

This tells you that the trains were a total of 50 minutes late over the five days Monday to Friday.

☐ Mode

> The **mode** is the most common, or most popular, data value.
>
> It is sometimes called the **modal value**.

The mode is the value that occurs most often, **not** the number of times that value occurs. So the modal value is not 2.

Example

For Jenny's results the modal value for the number of minutes the train is late is 8 min. The train was 8 min late on more days than any other value.

8 minutes appears twice.
8 minutes is the mode.

☐ Median

> The **median** is the middle value when the data is arranged in order. Usually you start with the smallest.

Example

Jenny's results are arranged in order like this:

    4   8   ⑧   13   17

The middle number is 8.

So the median number of minutes Jenny's train is late is 8 minutes.

Jenny recorded the number of minutes her train was late during a second week and wrote down these values:

    Mon 18 min   Tues 5 min   Wed 12 min

    Thur 14 min   Fri   9 min.

To find the median number of minutes the train was late over the two weeks, you must write down the ten values in order.

  4   5   8   8   ⟨9   12⟩   13   14   17   18

This time there are two numbers in the middle, 9 and 12.

To find the median, add the two numbers together and then divide by 2.

$$\text{Median} = \frac{9 + 12}{2} = 11.5 \text{ min.}$$

Notes

You can only work out the median after you have arranged the numbers in order.

If there is only one number in the middle then that is the median.

When there are two numbers in the middle, you must add these numbers together then divide by two to find the median.

This finds the value that is halfway between the two middle values.

Unit 10 pages 228–231 ⟩

TEST YOURSELF

1 Peter's homework marks over the last six weeks were:

Maths	65	78	70	54	73	68
Science	59	44	52	54	58	48
English	49	57	62	52	63	59

    a Work out the mean, median and range for each subject.

    b Which was Peter's best subject? Give a reason for your answer.

☐ Means and modes from tables

This table shows the number of pupils in each form at Riverdean School.

Number of pupils	Number of forms
25	4
26	1
27	5
28	8
29	9
30	3
Total	**30**

This table is called a frequency table.

To find the mean number of pupils per form you must add two extra columns to the table.

No. of pupils	No. of forms	Working: pupils × forms	Total number of pupils
25	4	4 × 25	100
26	1	1 × 26	26
27	5	5 × 27	135
28	8	8 × 28	224
29	9	9 × 29	261
30	3	3 × 30	90
Total	**30**		**836**

There are 4 forms each with 25 pupils, so the number of pupils on the first row is 100. There is only one form with 26 pupils, so this row only has 1 × 26 pupils.

To find the mean you work out $836 \div 30 = 27.866\ldots$

The mean number of pupils per form is 28 to the nearest person.

You can see from the table that there are more forms with 29 pupils than any other number. This is the modal value.

You must add up
$100 + 26 + 135 + 224 + 261 + 90 = 836$.
This tells you that there are 836 pupils altogether in the school.

Remember the mode is the most common value.

Unit 12 pages 277–282

TEST YOURSELF

1 Chloe carried out a survey to find the number of children in a family. Her results are given in the table.

No. of children	No. of families
0	3
1	8
2	11
3	4
4	2
5	2
Total	**30**

Find the mean number of children per family.

2 Simon throws a four-sided dice 50 times. The table shows the scores he obtained.

Score	No. of times thrown
1	14
2	12
3	13
4	11
Total	**50**

a Find the mean score on the dice.
b What was the modal score?

Probability

☐ Probability scales

Probability tells you how likely something is to happen.

Words such as impossible, very likely, unlikely are often used to describe probability.

Numbers are used to measure probability more accurately.

An event that is impossible has a probability of 0.

An event that is certain to happen has a probability of 1.

All probabilities are measured on a scale ranging from 0 to 1.

☐ Fair and unfair

In probability something is **fair** if it is no more or no less likely to happen than any other event.

If a coin is described as fair you would expect to have the same chance of getting a head as of getting a tail when the coin is thrown.

This spinner is not fair as you would be more likely to get red than blue.

Notes

The probability that the sun will rise tomorrow is certain. It is 1.

There is an even chance that you will get a head when a coin is thrown. The probability of this is 0.5 or $\frac{1}{2}$.

It is certain that October will come after September. The probability of this event is 1.

Unit 5 pages 102–105 ⟶

TEST YOURSELF

1 Draw a probability scale with numbers. Mark on it points **a**, **b** and **c** to show how likely you think each one is.

   a The score on a six-sided dice will be an even number.

   b The score will be four.

   c The score will be seven.

2 Jack and Lucy are playing a game. They throw a dice to see who goes first. Jack says he will go first if the number is a prime number. Lucy can go first if the number is not prime. Is this fair? Explain your answer.

☐ Adds up to one

Probabilities always add up to one.

If the probability that you will be set homework tonight is 80%, this means that there is a 20% chance you will not have homework.

80% is the same as $\frac{80}{100}$, and 20% is the same as $\frac{20}{100}$

Example

Joe has 5 blue counters and 3 green counters in a bag. He picks one out of the bag without looking. What is the probability that he picks a blue counter?

There are 8 counters altogether. So you can draw a scale marked in $\frac{1}{8}$ ths.

The probability that he picks a blue counter is $\frac{5}{8}$.

The probability that he picks a green counter is therefore $\frac{3}{8}$.

This is also the probability of **not** picking blue.

☐ Equally likely outcomes

Two events are **equally likely** if they have the same chance of happening.

When you throw a fair coin you are equally likely to get a head, as you are to get a tail.

Yellow and green are equally likely on this spinner.

☐ Probability of an event

You can use equally likely events to work out probabilities.

The **probability of an event A** is:

Number of ways that event A can happen
_____
Total number of outcomes

Notes

You can write probabilities as fractions, decimals or percentages.

$80\% + 20\% = 100\%$

$\frac{80}{100} + \frac{20}{100} = \frac{100}{100} = 1$

$\frac{5}{8} + \frac{3}{8} = 1$

Unit 7 pages 160–166

On this spinner there are six sections. Three are shaded yellow and three are green. There are the same number of green sections as there are yellow.

Outcomes are all the different events that can happen.

If you roll a fair dice like this:

there are six possible numbers that you could get:

1, 2, 3, 4, 5 or 6

The probability of getting a $4 = \dfrac{1}{6}$

The probability of getting a number less than 3

$= \dfrac{2}{6} = \dfrac{1}{3}$

Notes

There is only one 4 out of six possible outcomes.

The only numbers less than 3 are 1 and 2. So two out of the six possible scores are less than 3.

☐ Two-way tables

Sometimes you are given information in a table.

Example

Aarti carried out a survey to find how many students in Year 11 are left-handed. Her results are given in the table.

	Male	Female
Right-handed	66	72
Left-handed	12	10

Find the probability that a student selected at random is:

a female

b a left-handed male.

First you need to work out how many students there are altogether.

Add 66 + 72 + 12 + 10 = 160

a The number of female students is 72 + 10 = 82

So the probability of choosing a female $= \dfrac{82}{160}$

b There are 12 left-handed male students.

The probability that the student is a left-handed male

$= \dfrac{12}{100}$

In this table the number 72 tells you that there are 72 right-handed female students in the year.

Unit 11 pages 255–259

TEST YOURSELF

1 a What is the probability of getting yellow when this spinner is spun?

  b What is the probability of getting green?

  c What is the probability of not getting red?

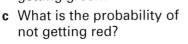

2 You have 4 red counters and 5 blue counters in a bag. You choose one counter at random. What is the probability that you choose a red counter?

3 The table shows the number of tickets sold at a local railway station.

	Adult	Child
Single	32	14
Return	56	28

Find the probability that one of these passengers chosen at random will be:

a a child; **b** an adult with a return ticket.

Relative frequency

The **relative frequency** of an event is the number of times that it happens divided by the total number of events that happen.

$$\text{Relative frequency} = \frac{\text{frequency}}{\text{total frequency}}$$

You can use relative frequency to estimate the probability of events which are not equally likely.

Example

Sanjay thinks that the coin he has been given is biased.

He throws the coin 80 times and gets 50 heads.

What is the relative frequency of heads?

$$\text{Relative frequency} = \frac{50}{80}$$

Sample space diagrams

A **sample space diagram** is a table which shows all the outcomes in a probability experiment.

If you roll a four-sided dice and throw a 20 p coin, then you could show all the possible outcomes in a table like this.

Score on dice	1	2	3	4
Head	H, 1	H, 2	H, 3	H, 4
Tail	T, 1	T, 2	T, 3	T, 4

There are 8 possible outcomes altogether.

T, 3 means the outcome is a Tail on the coin and a 3 on the dice.

The probability of getting a Tail and a 3 $= \frac{1}{8}$.

Notes

An event is something that happens in a probability experiment.

The frequency of an event is the number of times that it happens.

Relative frequency gives you a better estimate of probability the more times you do the experiment.

A coin which is biased is not a fair coin. That means that heads and tails are not equally likely.

Unit 16 pages 372–374

Outcomes are all the different events that can happen.

Unit 18 page 417

These 8 outcomes are equally likely.

There is only one outcome which gives both a Tail and a 3.

TEST YOURSELF

1 A biased dice is thrown 100 times. This table shows the results. Work out the relative frequency of each score.

Score	1	2	3	4	5	6
Frequency	12	14	25	20	14	15

2 Michael plays football and he keeps a record of the number of times he scores from the penalty spot during training. Here is his record.

Scores	Misses
25	11

a Estimate the probability he will score on his next attempt.

b Estimate the probability that he will miss on his next attempt.

Diagrams

☐ Tally-tables

You use a **tally-table** to show the results of experiments or surveys.

You always write tally-marks in groups of five.

Number of students who watched particular TV channels

Channel	Tally	Frequency
BBC1	JHT JHT JHT JHT	20
ITV	JHT JHT JHT JHT JHT JHT	30
Channel 4	JHT JHT	10
Channel 5	JHT JHT JHT	15
Sky	JHT JHT JHT JHT JHT	25

Remember that the fifth tally-mark is drawn across the first four, like this:

JHT

This makes it easier to count the tally-marks to find the frequency.

Unit 1 pages 10–13

☐ Reading charts

You can get a lot of information from a table of data, but graphs and charts are more interesting. You will find it is easier to understand data when they are shown on a graph or chart.

A **bar-chart** is made up of a series of bars. The height of each bar shows how many of each type there are.

Example

One hundred students were asked which TV channel they watched last night. This bar-chart shows the number of students who watched each TV channel.

a What was the most popular channel?

b How many students watched Channel 5?

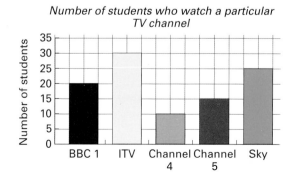

Number of students who watch a particular TV channel

a The most popular channel was ITV.
This is because the ITV bar is the highest.

b 15 people watched Channel 5.

A bar-chart has spaces between the bars.

Make sure you read the scale carefully.

The least popular channel was Channel 4. It has the lowest bar.

A **pictogram** uses pictures instead of bars.

Example

You could show the data on the bar chart with this pictogram.

BBC 1   ☐ ☐ ☐ ☐

ITV   ☐ ☐ ☐ ☐ ☐ ☐

Channel 4   ☐ ☐

Channel 5   ☐ ☐ ☐

Sky   ☐ ☐ ☐ ☐ ☐

Key: ☐ = 5 people

Check how many people, or objects, each picture represents.

Here ☐ represents 5 people.

Always give a pictogram a key.

Unit 3 pages 66–67

☐ **Drawing charts**

When you draw bar-charts use a ruler so that all lines are straight. You should leave a gap between each bar.

A **frequency polygon** is sometimes drawn instead of a bar-chart. You plot the values as points, then you join the points with straight lines.

Remember always to use a sharp pencil and a ruler for drawing all types of chart or graph. Your diagrams will look much neater.

Always give your chart a title and label both the axes. Show the scale you have used clearly. Choose a scale that gives a sensible size of graph.

Example

The mathematics GCSE results at Riverdean School last year were:

Grade	A*	A	B	C	D	E	F	G
%	2	6	24	22	21	15	7	3

Plot the percentage values at the correct height for each grade. Join the points together with straight lines.

In a frequency polygon the points are plotted in the middle of where the top of the bar would be.

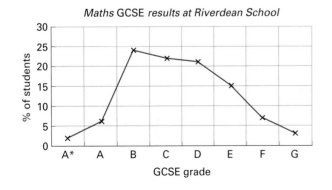

Maths GCSE results at Riverdean School

You can see immediately that there are more B grades than any other grade.

Unit 4 pages 78–84

☐ Line graphs

> **Discrete data** can only take certain values.
> The number of cars in a car park is an example of discrete data – you cannot have 27.5 cars!
>
> You can show discrete data on a **vertical line graph**. This looks like a bar-chart with lines instead of bars.

Example

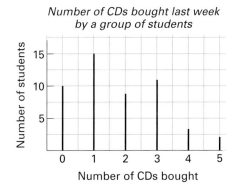

Number of CDs bought last week by a group of students

> **Continuous data** can take any value within a given range. The distance walked in a sponsored walk is an example of continuous data.
>
> Continuous data can be shown on a **line graph**, where all the points are joined together with straight lines.

Example

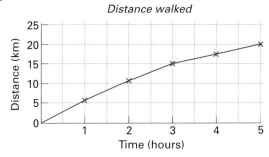

Distance walked

Continuous data can take any value on a scale.

If the sponsored walk is 25 km then someone could have walked 22.5 km or 23.9 km at any given time. In fact they can walk any distance between 0 and 25 km.

Unit 6 page 131 ⟹

TEST YOURSELF

1 Here are the marks scored by 30 students in a mental arithmetic test.

6	8	2	10	3	7	6	8	9	7
9	8	5	9	3	9	7	6	8	4
6	5	8	4	7	8	8	10	8	9

  a Draw a tally-chart for this data.
  b Show this data on a vertical line graph.

2 The temperatures recorded at Riverdean last summer were:

60	62	68	65	68	70	71	69	71	71
69	68	67	66	67	72	69	70	72	66
66	72	70	71	69	65	67	66	66	69
69	70	70	71	68	66	69	68	67	72
70	69	68	68	70	70	72	73	69	69
70	67	68	67	68	71	69	69	68	66

  a Draw a tally-chart for these temperatures.
  b Show this data on a bar-chart.

☐ Pie-charts

A **pie-chart** shows how something has been divided up. The angle of each slice represents the number of each item.

Example

The table gives the colours of cars in a car park.
Draw a pie-chart to show this data.

Black	Blue	Green	Red	Silver	White
21	18	13	20	8	10

Adding up:
21 + 18 + 13 + 20 + 8 + 10 = 90

There are 90 cars altogether. The angles at the centre of the circle add to 360°.

So each car is represented by 360° ÷ 90 = 4°.

Working out the angles for each slice gives:

If there were 180 cars, each car would be shown by 360 + 180 = 2°.

If there were 120 cars, each car would be shown by 360 ÷ 120 = 3°.

Colour	Working	Angles
Black	21 × 4°	84°
Blue	18 × 4°	72°
Green	13 × 4°	52°
Red	20 × 4°	80°
Silver	8 × 4°	32°
White	10 × 4°	40°

Check that your angles add up to 360°.

You can now draw the pie-chart

1 Draw a circle and mark the centre. Draw a line from the centre to the top of the circle. Draw the first angle of 84°.

2 Measure the next angle from the one you have just drawn.

3 Carry on until you have drawn all the angles.

Label each slice and don't forget a title.

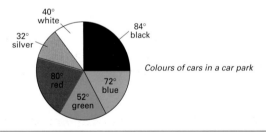

Colours of cars in a car park

Unit 9 pages 206–210

T E S T   Y O U R S E L F

1 Draw a pie-chart to show how Steven spends his money each week.

Spending	Rent	Food	Clothes	Bus	Other
Amount	£65	£50	£20	£15	£30

2 A survey to find out how pupils travelled to school produced the following results. Draw a pie-chart to show this data.

Method of travel	Walk	Cycle	Bus	Car
Number of pupils	250	50	270	150

☐ Scatter graphs

You use **scatter graphs** to see if there is a connection or correlation between two sets of data.

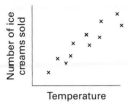

This shows positive correlation. As the temperature increases so does the sale of ice creams.

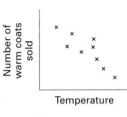

This shows negative correlation. As the temperature increases the sale of warm coats decreases.

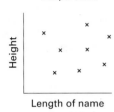

This shows zero correlation. There is no connection between the length of a student's name and their height.

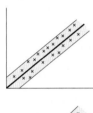

These points lie close to the line of best fit. The correlation is strong.

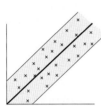

These points are well spread out from the line of best fit, but still follow the trend. The correlation is weak.

> **Unit 8** pages 183–186

Notes

Correlation is a measure of how strongly two sets of data are connected.

In an exam question you may be asked to comment on the relationship between two sets of data. Try to use some of the words given here.

One value goes on the x-axis and the other goes on the y-axis.
It does not matter which way round they go unless you are told!

The first student scored 45 in French and 50 in German. This is shown by plotting a point at (45, 50).

If two sets of data show correlation you can use your scatter graph to estimate missing values.
First you must draw a line which goes through the middle of the points. This is called the *line of best fit*. It is the line in red. You can use this line to estimate data values.

Example

Here are the test scores for a group of students taking French and German.

French	45	56	58	63	74	58	62	42	39	45
German	50	58	56	62	76	53	63	46	35	43

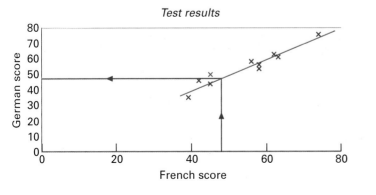

You can estimate the German score of a student who scored 48 in French but was absent for the German test.

1 Find the score of 48 on the French axis.
2 Draw a straight line (blue) up to the red line.
3 Now draw a horizontal line (blue) to the German axis.
4 You can read off the value on the German axis.

You can see that the estimate for the German mark is 48.

☐ Misleading graphs

> Graphs are used to make data easier to understand.
>
> Sometimes graphs are deliberately drawn to mislead.
>
> Always check the scales of graphs, including pictograms.
>
> The most common 'error' is to show scales which do not start at zero.

Notes

Unit 17 pages 386–390

Misleading graphs often have no scales, or scales which are inaccurate.

Unit 14 pages 327–330

TEST YOURSELF

1 The table gives the weights and heights of 15 boys.

Draw a scatter graph for the data. Estimate the weight of a boy who is 160 cm tall.

Height (cm)	158	159	157	165	161	162	159	160	164	156	159	162	170	157	155
Weight (kg)	60	61	63	66	59	62	58	60	62	60	57	61	65	56	58

2 The table gives the results of 10 pupils in Geography and History tests.

Draw a scatter graph for these results. Is there any correlation between these results?

Geography (%)	68	90	42	50	86	84	78	80	50	65
History (%)	60	85	40	41	75	89	65	78	46	80

3 Explain why this graph is misleading.

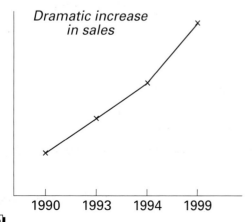

Practice questions

1 Alan throws a fair coin 600 times.

    a How many times would you expect him to get Heads?   *(1)*

Here is a 5-sided spinner

Its sides are labelled 1, 2, 3, 4, 5.

Alan spins the spinner and throws a coin.
One possible outcome is (3, Heads).

    b List all the possible outcomes.   *(2)*

The spinner is biased.
The probability that the spinner will land on each of the numbers 1 to 4
is given in the table.

Number	1	2	3	4	5
Probability	0.36	0.1	0.25	0.15	

Alan spins the spinner once.

    c **i**   Work out the probability that the spinner will land on 5.

         ii Write down the probability that the spinner will land on 6.

        iii Write down the number that the spinner is most likely to land on.   *(4)*

Edexcel, 1999, Paper 1

2 Nicky recorded the numbers of people getting off her bus at 10 stops.
Here are her results.

        2   4   3   6   3   6   3   7   11   8

For these 10 numbers, work out:

    a the mean   *(3)*

    b the median   *(2)*

    c the range.   *(2)*

Edexcel, 1999, Paper 1

3 In a survey a researcher asks 72 people to name their favourite types of television
programmes.

The results are shown in the table below.

Type of programme	Soaps	Drama	Comedy	Sport
Frequency	40	4	10	18

Draw a pie-chart to the distribution of the results. **You must show how you calculate the
angles of your pie-chart.**   *(4)*

WJEC, 1999, Paper 1

ANSWERS

Numbers

Place value, page 3

1 a Eight thousand nine hundred and forty five
b Forty thousand five hundred and one
c Two hundred and four thousand and ninety seven
d Seven million four hundred thousand and seventy six

2 a 254 729   **b** 3 002 004

3 a 37, 347, 429, 492, 4091
b 29.357, 29.375, 29.457

4 a 270   **b** 76.1   **c** 4235.6

5 a 3200   **b** 250.9   **c** 2482

6 a 68000   **b** 8073   **c** 36800

7 a 790   **b** 429   **c** 60.07

8 a 43   **b** 24.7   **c** 6.091

page 4

1 a 1000   1400
b 1500   2100
c 2500   3500
d 750   1050
e 2100   2940
f 3350   4690

2 a 6000   120 000
b 120 000   2 400 000
c 201 000   4 020 000

3 a 5   **b** 20   **c** 31
d 50   **e** 150   **f** 220

4 a 4   **b** 15   **c** 230

4 rules of number, page 5

1 a 6, 12, 18, 24, 30, 36, 42, 48, 54, 60
b 7, 14, 21, 28, 35, 42, 49, 56, 63, 70
c 8, 16, 24, 32, 40, 48, 56, 64, 72, 80
d 9, 18, 27, 36, 45, 54, 63, 72, 81, 90

2
1, 2, 3, 4, 5, 6, 7, 8, 9, 10
2, 4, 6, 8, 10, 12, 14, 16, 18, 20
3, 6, 9, 12, 15, 18, 21, 24, 27, 30
4, 8, 12, 16, 20, 24, 28, 32, 36, 40
5, 10, 15, 20, 25, 30, 35, 40, 45, 50
6, 12, 18, 24, 30, 36, 42, 48, 54, 60
7, 14, 21, 28, 35, 42, 49, 56, 63, 70
8, 16, 24, 32, 40, 48, 56, 64, 72, 80
9, 18, 27, 36, 45, 54, 63, 72, 81, 90
10, 20, 30, 40, 50, 60, 70, 80, 90, 100

page 7

1 a 972   **b** 5560
c 12397   **d** 11568

2 a 145   **b** 379
c 116   **d** 3137

3 a 1296   **b** 2516   **c** 16536
d 26523   **e** 10660   **f** 63412
g 409 133

4 a 117   **b** 63   **c** 876
d 12   **e** 234   **f** 67

page 8

1 a 9.48   **b** 10.13
c £50.64   **d** 287.036 kg

2 a 2.55   **b** 2.64 m

3 a 7.62   **b** 445.74   **c** 1.392
d 37.71   **e** 4.404   **f** 8.208
g 0.441

4 a 1.43   **b** 8.43   **c** 64.5

page 10

1 a 16, 18, 20, 22, 24, 26
b 325, 327, 329, 331, 333, 335
c 6, 12, 18, 24, 30, 36
d 36, 45, 54, 63
e 1, 2, 4, 5, 10, 20
f 1, 2, 3, 4, 6, 9, 12, 18, 36
g 31   37
h 21, 28, 36, 45
i 49, 64, 81, 100, 121

2 a prime number
b multiples (of 3 between 9 and 21)
c triangle numbers
d square numbers
e factors (of 18)
f multiples (of 2 between 8 and 16) or even numbers
g square root
h odd numbers

Negative numbers, page 12

1 −162, −53, −11, −6

2 −4 099, −2 086, −409, −208, −206

3 a −2   **b** −2   **c** −10
d −23   **e** 2   **f** −15

4 a 3   **b** −16   **c** −5
d −38   **e** −47   **f** −665

Fractions, page 14

1 **a** 11   **b** 7   **c** 9
    d 9   **e** 8   **f** 7
    g 9   **h** 8   **i** 30

2 **a** 14   **b** 24   **c** 18
    d 10   **e** 30   **f** 304
    g 60   **h** 672   **i** 128

3 **a** $\frac{3}{2}$ **b** $\frac{8}{3}$ **c** $\frac{15}{4}$
    d $\frac{17}{5}$ **e** $\frac{29}{6}$ **f** $\frac{79}{16}$

4 **a** $5\frac{1}{2}$ **b** $4\frac{2}{3}$ **c** $3\frac{1}{7}$

5 **a** $\frac{1}{2} = \frac{4}{8}$ **b** $\frac{3}{8} = \frac{6}{16}$ **c** $\frac{4}{5} = \frac{8}{10}$
    d $\frac{3}{7} = \frac{6}{14}$ **e** $\frac{14}{25} = \frac{56}{100}$ **f** $\frac{8}{9} = \frac{320}{360}$

page 15

1 **a** $\frac{2}{4} = \frac{1}{2}$ **b** $\frac{6}{8} = \frac{3}{4}$ **c** $\frac{10}{16} = \frac{5}{8}$
    d $\frac{4}{16} = \frac{1}{4}$ **e** $\frac{3}{12} = \frac{1}{4}$ **f** $\frac{6}{9} = \frac{2}{3}$
    g $\frac{5}{20} = \frac{1}{4}$ **h** $\frac{10}{25} = \frac{2}{5}$ **i** $\frac{8}{24} = \frac{1}{3}$

2 **a** $\frac{1}{2}$ **b** $\frac{1}{2}$ **c** $1\frac{1}{2}$
    d $\frac{5}{8}$ **e** $1\frac{2}{3}$ **f** $\frac{3}{5}$
    g $\frac{2}{7}$ **h** $\frac{3}{4}$ **i** $\frac{1}{3}$

3 **a** $1\frac{1}{4}$ **b** $\frac{7}{16}$ **c** $1\frac{1}{16}$
    d $\frac{3}{10}$ **e** $1\frac{1}{2}$ **f** $\frac{13}{20}$
    g $\frac{1}{6}$ **h** $1\frac{1}{40}$ **i** $\frac{17}{63}$

4 **a** $3\frac{3}{4}$ **b** $2\frac{3}{16}$ **c** $9\frac{1}{6}$
    d $3\frac{1}{2}$ **e** $9\frac{11}{20}$ **f** $1\frac{10}{21}$

Percentages, page 17

1 **a** 22%   **b** 30%   **c** 3%   **d** 99%

2 **a** $\frac{40}{100}$ **b** $\frac{4}{100}$ **c** $\frac{88}{100}$ **d** $\frac{47}{100}$

3 **a** £80   **b** £32.40

4 **a** £1170   **b** £5059.20   **c** £1376

page 19

1 **a** £17.50   **b** £10.50   **c** £43.75
    d £5.60   **e** £787.50   **f** £168.88

2 **a** £4760   **b** £39.67

3 **a** 20%   **b** 32%   **c** 16%
    d 100%   **e** 85%   **f** 16.67%

4 **a** 40%   **b** 38%   **c** 13%
    d 33%   **e** 3%   **f** 26.04% 2dp

Linking fractions, decimals and percentages, page 20

1 **a** 0.6   **b** 0.25   **c** 0.667 3d.p.
    d 0.375

2 **a** 9%   **b** 76%

3 **a** 40%   **b** 75%   **c** 87.5%
    d 71.4% (to 1d.p.)

page 21

1 **a** $\frac{3}{10}$ **b** $\frac{7}{10}$ **c** $\frac{1}{100}$ **d** $\frac{8}{100} = \frac{2}{25}$
    e $\frac{47}{100}$ **f** $\frac{75}{100} = \frac{3}{4}$ **g** $\frac{66}{100} = \frac{33}{50}$ **h** $\frac{8}{1000} = \frac{1}{125}$

2 **a** 0.25   **b** 0.70   **c** 0.07   **d** 0.77

3 **a** $\frac{1}{4}$ **b** $\frac{4}{10} = \frac{2}{5}$ **c** $\frac{65}{100} = \frac{13}{20}$ **d** $\frac{24}{100} = \frac{8}{25}$

4 $0.84 = \frac{21}{25}$ $0.42 = \frac{21}{50} = 42\%$

Ratio, page 23

1   5 : 1

2   6 kg

3   the 180 g packet is better value

4 **a** 64p   **b** £1.28   **c** 28 rolls

Rounding, page 24

1 **a** 40   **b** 60   **c** 80
    d 10   **e** 60   **f** 100

2 **a** 700   **b** 800   **c** 800
    d 200   **e** 800   **f** 1000

3 **a** 2000   **b** 4000   **c** 5000

4 **a** 12.7 cm   **b** 84.2 cm   **c** 17.4 km

5 **a** 68.42 g   **b** 4.37 t   **c** 0.09 kg

page 25

1 **a** 4   **b** 7   **c** 3

2 **a** 20   **b** 6   **c** 50
    d 600   **e** 9000   **f** 0.3

3 **a** 2.3   **b** 0.0699   **c** 48.9   **d** 54700

4

	Actual	Estimate
a	31.92	32
b	7.26 2d.p.	8
c	16.8	17
d	6.28	6
e	32352	35000
f	44.66 2d.p.	40

Changing currencies, page 26

1 a $15.80 **b** $34.76 **c** $1 200.80

2 a £200 **b** £45 **c** £122.50

3 a 4 **b** 4.5

BODMAS, page 28

1 a 14 **b** 14 **c** 8
  d 4 **e** 22 **f** 8

2 a 28 **b** 4 **c** −2
  d 64 **e** 1

3 a 36 **b** 125 **c** 256
  d 256 **e** 5625 **f** 3136

4 a 3^4 **b** $9^3 \times 2^2$

5 a 100000 **b** 10368 **c** 512

Standard form, page 29

1 a 5×10^8 **b** 9.6×10^{17}
  c 6.093×10^{12} **d** 6×10^9
  e 1.48×10^{22} **f** 2.007×10^{18}

2 a 2×10^{10} **b** 2.4×10^{11}
  c 1.512×10^{11} **d** 9×10^{11}

3 a 4.8×10^{11} **b** 1.078×10^{18}
  c 6.57×10^{29} **d** 2×10^1
  c 3×10^3 **d** 2.55×10^{21} 2d.p.

Practice questions

1 a i) $5 \times 60\% = 5 \times 0.6 = 3.0$ kg.
  So a large bag weighs $5 + 3 = 8$ kg *(2)*

  ii) In 3:4, the 3 shares are the 96p
  So each share $= 96 \div 3 = 32$p.
  So 4 shares $= 32 \times 4 = 128$p. *(3)*

b 3 kg cost 72p so each kg costs
  $72 \div 3 = 24$p
  14 kg cost £2.66 so each kg costs
  $266 \div 14 = 19$p
  So 5p per kg is saved by buying sacks *(3)*

2 a £18 ≈ £20 148 days ≈ 150 days
  $150 \times 20 = £3000$
  [or £18 ≈ £20 148 days ≈ 100 days
  then $100 \times 20 = £2000$] *(3)*

b
```
      148
   ×   18
    1184
    1480
         ³⁶
    2664        Answer = £2664   (3)
```

3
$$R = \frac{ph}{5}$$

$$R = \frac{15.5 \times 2.25}{5}$$

So R = 6.975
So Carol will need to buy 7 complete rolls *(3)*

Algebra

Formulas, page 33

1 40 km

2 a $w = 8 + 5n$ **b** £68

3 31.3

4 a 4 **b** p = 10

5 250

Patterns, page 34

1 a $10n$ **b** 200

2 a $7n$ **b** 140

3 a $9n$ **b** 180

4 a $\frac{1}{2}n$ **b** 5 **c** 25

page 35

1 a 1 6 11 **b** 396 **c** 32nd term

2 a $3n + 4$ **b** $6n - 2$ **c** $10n + 3$

page 36

1 a
  b 3 5 7 9 **c** $2n + 1$ **d** 25 sticks **e** 88th

2 a
  b $2n + 3$ **c** 40th pattern **d** 113 counters

Equations, page 37

1 a $m = 3$ **b** $x = 16$ **c** $h = 5$

2 a $m = 4$ **b** $x = 7$ **c** $y = 24$ **d** $x = 6$

page 39

1 a i $6x - 12$ **ii** $4x$
  b $6x - 12 = 4x$ **c** $x = 6$

2 a $3t$ **b** $9xy + 5y$
  c $2b^2$ **d** $4x^2 + 2x$

3 a $6y + 12$ **b** $12d - 15$
  c $8m - 4$ **d** $21x - 28y$

4 a 33 **b** 23

Graphs, page 42

1 a b

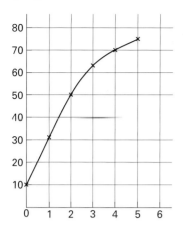

c i 40°C   **ii** $2\frac{1}{2}$ minutes

Practice questions

1 $C = 65n$ *(2)*

2 a $x = 3$ *(2)*   **b** $x = -20$ *(1)*   **c** $z = 11$ *(3)*

3 a i square numbers *(1)*
   ii 36 *(1)*
 b i 42 white tiles *(1)*
   ii 65 black tiles *(1)*

Shape, space and measures

2D Shapes, page 47

1 a

Right angled triangle

b

Isosceles triangle

c

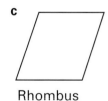

Rhombus

d

Trapezium

2 a A regular triangle is an **equilateral** triangle

  b A regular quadrilateral is a **square**.

---

3 a

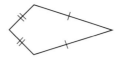

b

c

d

e

page 48

1 A and G
  B and E
  C and F
  D and I

2 a

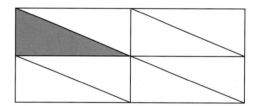

b

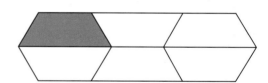

3D Shapes, page 50

1 a 5   **b** 8   **c** 5

2 a cone   **b** regular hexagonal prism.

3 a

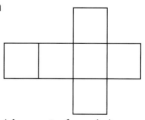

(*Any net of a cube*)

b

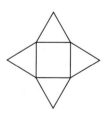

c

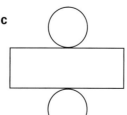

(*Length of rectangle must be $\pi \times$ diameter of circles*)

4

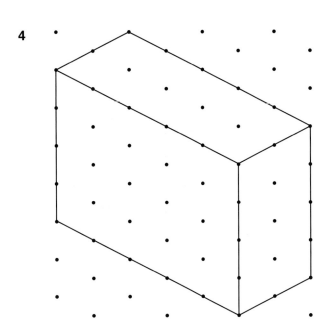

b

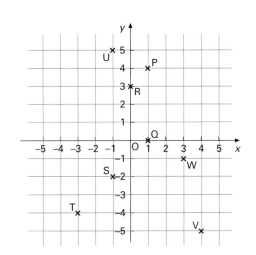

Symmetry, page 52

1

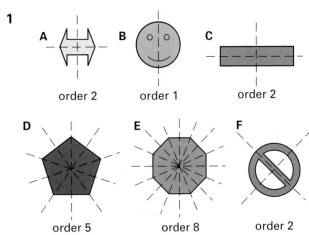

A — order 2 B — order 1 C — order 2

D — order 5 E — order 8 F — order 2

2

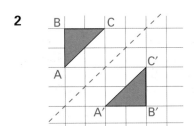

3 a

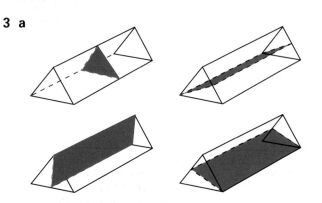

Co-ordinates, page 53

1 **A** (2, 1)   **B** (0, 3)   **C** (–5, 1)
   D (–3, 4)   **E** (–4, –1)   **F** (–3, –4)
   G (4, –2)   **H** (1, –4)

2

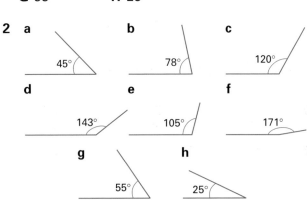

Angles, page 54

1 **A** 35°   **B** 82°   **C** 125°
   D 155°   **E** 145°   **F** 98°
   G 55°   **H** 25°

2 **a**   **b**   **c**
   45°   78°   120°

   d   **e**   **f**
   143°   105°   171°

      g   **h**
      55°   25°

   a 45°   **b** 78°   **c** 120°
   d 143°   **e** 105°   **f** 171°
   g 270°   **h** 230°

1 a a = 180 – 81
a = 99°

b b = 360 – 160 – 123
b = 77°

c c = 180° – 93 – 64
c = 23°

d d = 360° – 100 – 80 – 95
d = 85°

e e = 72°
f = g = 108°

f 2h = 180 – 70
= 110°
h = 55°

g i = 360° – 90 – 90 – 81
i = 99°

h j = 130°
k = 180° – 130 – 30
k = 20°

page 57

1 a a = d = g = 40°
b = c = e = f = 140°

b q = u = t = 130°
p = r = s = v = 50°

c i = 180 – 105 = 75°
j = 180 – 50 = 130°

d $\frac{360}{5}$ = 72° x = 180 – 72 = 108°

e y = $\frac{360}{8}$ = 45° z = 180 – 45° = 135°

f l = $\frac{360}{10}$ = 36° m = 180 – 36 = 144°

2 a 90° **b** 45° **c** 135°
d 135° **e** 135° **f** 90°

3 a 062° **b** 165° **c** 245° **d** 330°

Transformations, page 59

1

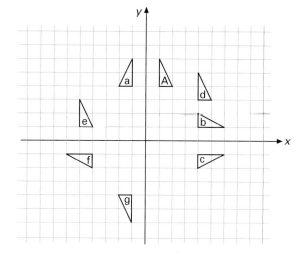

2 a F **b** E **c** B
d D **e** A **f** C

Measures, page 61

1 a 5.1 amps **b** 2.46 g

2 clockwise from top
730 m
120 m
420 m
140 m
310 m
260 m

3 a pupils own drawing **b** 2760 m ± 15 m

4 pupils own drawing
angles are 30°, 94°, 56°

5 pupils own drawing

page 62

1 a 400 cm **b** 6200 m **c** 8.5 cm
d 7.8 km **e** 4.8 g **f** 2900 mg
g 94 tonnes **h** 5850 g **i** 0.45 l
j 2.3 l **k** 250 cl **l** 450 ml

2 a 10 cm **b** 5 ft **c** 10 miles
d 24 in **e** 120 g **f** 2 lb
g 65 kg **h** 8 oz **i** 3000 ml
j 27 l **k** 4 pt **l** 20 gal

page 64

1 Thursday 9th December

2 11.17

3 60 km/h

4 12 miles/s

5 a $\frac{1}{2}$ hr **b** 200 km/h fast train
40 km/h tube
80 km/h slow train

Perimeter, area and volume, page 65

1 a 6.3 m   **b** 1.5 m

2 a 90 m²   **b** 1.2 m²

page 67

1 a 78.5 cm   **b** 14.1 m   **c** 17.0 cm

2 a 50.27 cm²   **b** 940.25 m²   **c** 72.38 m²

3 a 601 m²

4 a 262.14 m³   **b** 50.4 m³

Practice questions

1 Area = 5 × 5 + 4 × 3
$$= 25 + 12 = 37 \text{ m}^2 \quad (4)$$

2 a $x = 65°$ (alternate angles)   *(2)*

   b $y = 70°$ (interior angles)   *(2)*

3 a Area of table = $\pi \times (2.35)^2$
$$= 17.349\ldots$$
17.349… ÷ 4 = 4.337… tins of varnish
So 5 litre tins are needed to paint the table   *(4)*

   b Circumference = $2 \times \pi \times 2.35$
$$= 14.765\ldots = 14.8 \text{ m (1dp)} \quad (2)$$

Handling data

Averages and range, page 71

1 a

	Mean	Median	Range
Maths	68	69	24
Science	52.5	53	15
English	57	58	14

   b Although the mean and median for maths is the highest the range is also the largest. English has the lowest range, which suggest greater consistency.

page 72

1 Mean is 2 children per family

2 a mean score is 2.42
   b modal score is 1

Probability, page 73

1

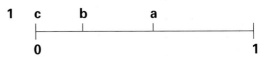

2 a Probability of a prime number is $\frac{1}{2}$. Probability of a number that is not prime is also $\frac{1}{2}$. This is fair as they have an equal chance.

page 75

1 a $\frac{1}{8}$ **b** $\frac{4}{8} = \frac{1}{2}$ **c** $\frac{5}{8}$

2 $\frac{4}{9}$

3 a $\frac{42}{130} = \frac{21}{65}$ **b** $\frac{56}{130} = \frac{28}{65}$

page 76

1 a

Score	1	2	3	4	5	6
Frequency	0.12	0.14	0.25	0.20	0.14	0.15

2 a $\frac{25}{36}$ **b** $\frac{11}{36}$

Diagrams, page 79

1 a

	Tally	Frequency
1		0
2		1
3		2
4		2
5		2
6		4
7		4
8		8
9		5
10		2

b

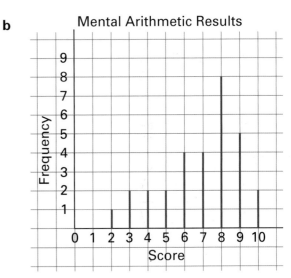

Mental Arithmetic Results

2 a

	Tally	Frequency
60	I	1
61		0
62	I	1
63		0
64		0
65	II	2
66	ЖТ II	7
67	ЖТ I	6
68	ЖТ ЖТ	10
69	ЖТ ЖТ II	12
70	ЖТ IIII	9
71	ЖТ I	6
72	ЖТ	5
73	I	1

b

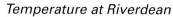
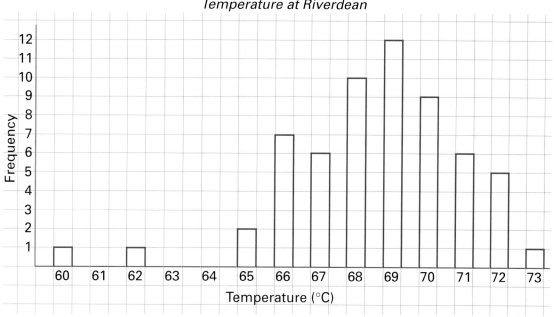

page 80

1

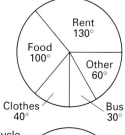

2

1 60.5 kg

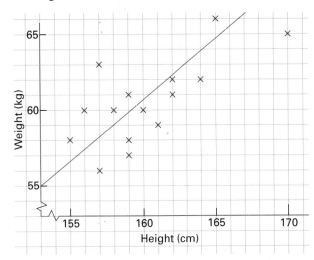

2 There is a positive correlation between the geography and history scores.

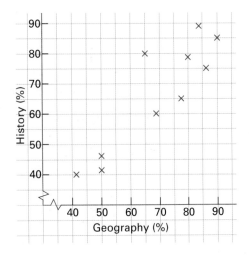

3 No scale on the vertical axis.
Scale on horizontal axis is not correct.

Practice questions

1 a 300 times   *(1)*

  b 1H   2H   3H   4H   5H
      1T   2T   3T   4T   5T   *(2)*

  c i 0.14   **ii** 0   **iii** 1 *(4)*

2 a 5.3   *(3)*   **b** 5   *(2)*   **c** 9   *(2)*

3

Soap	40 × 5°	200°
Drama	4 × 5°	20°
Comedy	10 × 5°	50°
Sport	18 × 5°	90°

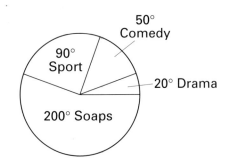